W9-CBW-024

Doing
Honest
Work in
College

· · · · · · · · · · · ·

Chicago Guides
to *Writing*, Editing,
and Publishing

Doing
Honest
Work in
College

. . . .

HOW TO PREPARE CITATIONS,

AVOID PLAGIARISM, AND ACHIEVE

REAL ACADEMIC SUCCESS

Charles Lipson

The University of Chicago Press CHICAGO AND LONDON

Charles Lipson

is professor and

director of

undergraduate

studies in political

science at the

University of

Chicago.

The University of Chicago Press, Chicago 60637
The University of Chicago Press, Ltd., London
© 2004 by Charles Lipson
All rights reserved. Published 2004
Printed in the United States of America

13 12 11 10 09 08 07 06 05 04   1 2 3 4 5

ISBN: 0-226-48472-6 (cloth)
ISBN: 0-226-48473-4 (paper)

Library of Congress Cataloging-in-Publication Data
Lipson, Charles.
    Doing honest work in college : how to prepare
citations, avoid plagiarism, and achieve real
academic success / Charles Lipson.
        p. cm. — (Chicago guides to writing,
editing, and publishing)
    Includes index.
    ISBN 0-226-48472-6 (alk. paper)
    ISBN 0-226-48473-4 (pbk. : alk. paper)
        1. Bibliographical citations. 2. Plagiarism.
    I. Title. II. Series.
    PN171.F56L56 2004
    025.3′24 — dc22

                                    2004007886

♾ The paper used in this publication meets the
minimum requirements of the American National
Standard for Information Sciences — Permanence of
Paper for Printed Library Materials, ANSI Z39.48-1992.

To the memory of

Dorothy Kohn Lipson

and Harry M. Lipson Jr.

Models of integrity

SIGNS OF THE TIMES

Number of Wisconsin accounting students
given take-home tests to accommodate an Enron
whistle-blower's April speech: 78
Number later found to have cheated: 40
— "Harper's Index," *Harper's Magazine*, July 2003

Google search: "Catcher in the Rye" + phony
Top two results: ready-to-use term papers on
the topic
— search on February 16, 2004

CONTENTS

. . . .

Academic Honesty

· · · · · · · · · · · · ·

THE THREE PRINCIPLES
OF ACADEMIC HONESTY

. . . .

Academic honesty boils down to three simple but powerful principles:

- When you say you did the work yourself, you actually did it.
- When you rely on someone else's work, you cite it. When you use their words, you quote them openly and accurately, and you cite them, too.
- When you present research materials, you present them fairly and truthfully. That's true whether the research involves data, documents, or the writings of other scholars.

These are bedrock principles, easy to remember and follow. They apply to all your classes, labs, papers, and exams. They apply to everyone in the university, from freshmen to professors. They're not just principles for students. They're principles for academic honesty across the entire university.

Of course, each university has its own code of conduct, and each class its own rules for specific assignments. In the next chapter, I'll discuss these detailed rules and explain how to follow them in papers, labs, study groups, and exams.

I'll also discuss how to use the Internet properly for assignments and show you how to cite Web pages, as well as books, articles, poems, films, and unpublished works. With this brief book, you can avoid plagiarism and handle nearly every citation you'll ever do, from anthropology to astrophysics.

Speaking of sciences, what about honesty in study groups and labs? That can be confusing because you sometimes work with fellow students and sometimes by yourself. What exactly are you supposed to do on your own, without any help? I'll pass along useful advice from lab supervisors, who explain how to use study groups more effectively and how to avoid any problems.

On all these issues, I'll report on conversations with deans of students. They deal with academic honesty every day and know the issues well. Believe me, it's a lot better to read their advice here than to have them explain it to you privately! That is a meeting you do *not* want to have.

The most important advice is to *listen* to your professors' rules for each assignment, *ask* for clarification if you're unsure, and then *follow the three basic principles*: If you say you did this work, then you really did it. If you quoted others or used their research, you acknowledge it openly. If you say the data or lab experiment came out a particular way, then it really did. Never make up data, hide bad results, or steal others' work. Don't misrepresent your findings or anyone else's. Don't misrepresent their ideas, either.

If you follow this straightforward advice, you'll stay on the right side of your university's rules and meet the highest standards of academic integrity. Your grades will be honestly earned.

Now, let's get down to nuts and bolts.

2

ACADEMIC HONESTY FROM YOUR FIRST CLASS TO YOUR FINAL EXAM

. . . .

What does it mean to do honest work in college? This chapter explores everyday issues that arise in college and offers practical solutions, beginning with reading assignments and exams. From the first day of classes, you'll be required to read books, articles, and electronic documents, so it's important to know what's expected. It's also important to know what's expected in seminars and discussion sections, as well as specialized classes such as foreign languages. I'll cover all of those and offer concrete advice.

Within a few weeks, you'll be taking midterm exams. Whether they are in-class or take-home, all exams share one basic rule: You have to do your own work, without "borrowing" from others. But beyond that, the rules vary. I'll discuss these different rules and explain what to do if you're unsure about them.

Next, I'll turn to one of the most important tasks in college, writing papers. Research for these papers requires you to draw on others' work and combine it with your own ideas. That means taking clear notes and using quotes and citations properly. I'll explain that in this chapter and the next, showing how to take notes that clearly separate your words and ideas from another author's. I'll explain how to quote and paraphrase in your papers and how to cite the works you rely on, whether they're in print or on the Web.

Readings, exams, and papers are all individual assignments. Other assignments, however, require you to work closely with fellow students. In chemistry and biology, for example, you'll work alongside a lab partner. In math and statistics, you may join a study group. What are you supposed to do together? And what are you supposed to do separately? I'll explain.

I'll also explain what to do about a low grade. One thing you can always do is get advice about how to do better next time. Teachers *want* to help students, especially those who want to improve and are willing to work at it. You can also appeal if you think your paper was graded too harshly. To do that, though, you need to follow some basic guidelines. You can't change anything on the paper or exam, and you should offer a clear, sensible reason for the appeal. I'll explain that later in the chapter.

Finally, I'll discuss honor codes, which some colleges use to encourage honest work and personal responsibility.

The aim of this chapter, then, is to give you an overview of what it means to do honest work in college and take you step-by-step through the issues you'll confront. I'll discuss reading assignments, exams, papers, study groups, and labs, and I'll offer some suggestions about problems that occasionally crop up. I'll also pass along some tips about studying more effectively. All these ideas point toward a single goal: honest learning.

READING ASSIGNMENTS

From the first day of class, you'll get reading assignments. It's a mistake to skip the reading — but it's not cheating. Some students read summaries (such as CliffsNotes) to supplement their readings or even to substitute for them. As a supplement they're fine, if you think they help. As a substitute, they shortchange your education. But you aren't violating any academic rules.

> *Tip on reading more efficiently:* Don't sit down, open an article or nonfiction book to the first page, and try to read it straight through. It helps to get an overview first. Look at the introduction, conclusion, and table of contents. If it's an article, read the abstract and section headings. Then read the introduction and conclusion. You don't have to keep the ending secret. It's not a mystery novel. After this overview, you'll have a good sense of the overall work and can begin more detailed reading.

EXAMS

Exams come in two delicious flavors: in-class and take-home. Because the formats are different, so are the rules governing them. Let's consider each briefly.

In-Class Exams

Most in-class exams are "closed book." They don't allow you to consult any materials, including handwritten notes or data stored on your computer or PDA. You might be asked to bring your own blue books to an exam — blank ones, of course. Those are the default rules for in-class exams, and they are rarely changed. Stick to them unless you are explicitly told otherwise. If you are unsure about a particular exam, simply ask your professor.

Along the same lines, you should not have access to an exam before it is given. You may be able to guess what's on the exam, and it's fine to look at last year's or last semester's. But current exams are off-limits until you take them.

Occasionally, teachers give open-book exams in class. Students can use their notes, thumb through their books, and type answers on their computers during the test (although not prior to it). That certainly cuts down on dull work and rote memorization, but it doesn't make the tests any easier. Students still need to know the material well so they can write compelling answers and, if necessary, find essential information quickly.

In one legendary test, a teacher explained that his next exam would be open book and students could use "anything they can carry into class." One carried in a graduate student. I highly recommend this approach. It cuts down on needless studying.

Actually, you have to write your exams without any help. That's true whether they are open or closed book. No glances at other students' papers. No downloading precooked answers from the Internet or from your own hard drive. No using others' words and ideas without proper quotes and citations. And, unfortunately, no carrying in graduate students, even very light ones.

> *Tip on in-class exams:* You can't use notes, books, articles, or electronic data when you write in-class exams, unless you are specifically told otherwise.

It's fine to study together before exams. Practicing answers is a great way to study — or, rather, it's great if you participate actively in the group. It doesn't help much if you just sit and listen. (That's one reason why small study groups are better than large ones.) Once you are inside the exam room, however, you are on your own. That's a central pillar of academic honesty.

Learn from Woody Allen's experience: "I was thrown out of NYU my freshman year for cheating on the metaphysics final. . . . I looked within the soul of the boy sitting next to me."[1]

Take-Home Exams

Take-home exams are usually open book. You are permitted to use books, articles, notes, and the Web. That's the standard policy, although it pays to check the rules for each exam.

Even if you are allowed to use published works and your own notes, you cannot ask others for help. That's cheating, just as it would be in class.

Similarly, if you incorporate ideas from books, articles, or the Web, you need to indicate that they are others' ideas. Even though it's an exam rather than a research paper, play it safe and cite any work you rely on. (Later, I'll show you exactly how to do that.) If it's a direct quote, enclose it in quotation marks and include a specific citation. If you've paraphrased something, use your own words, not a close imitation of the author's. And, of course, you still need to cite the original source.

Even with proper citations and quotes, the work has to be your own. You can't copy chunks of text off the Internet, drop them into your exam or research paper, pop in a citation or two, and call it your own. It's not. Cutting and pasting doesn't make it truly *your* exam or *your* paper. It's simply a patchwork quilt of others' work.

Actually, the rules are even more strict, for both exams and papers. You cannot copy as much as a single sentence — from the Web, a book, or anything else — *unless* you clearly mark it as a quote and cite it properly. Remember the basic principle: When you rely on someone else's work, you cite it; when you use their words, you quote them openly and accurately.

> *Tip on take-home exams:* You are usually permitted to use books, articles, notes, and the Web for take-home exams, although it always pays to check. What you can *never* do is copy answers or ask anyone for help. The exam is still yours alone to complete. Whatever sources you use, phrase the answers in your own words and cite the source. If you copy anything directly from these sources, place it in quotation marks and cite it.

---

1. The quote is from *Annie Hall*, DVD, directed by Woody Allen, written by Woody Allen and Marshall Brickman, MGM/UA Studios (1977; Santa Monica: MGM Home Video, 2003).

PAPERS

Paper assignments are almost always meant to be done individually. (Later, I'll discuss group assignments. For now, let's concentrate on individual work.) You need to do the reading, research, and writing by yourself and take responsibility for the results. It's great to talk about the project, and it's fine to consult teachers, writing tutors, and friends. Feel free to show them a draft version and get their feedback. But you need to do your own research, organize the paper, and write it yourself.

You will almost always utilize the work of others. That's essential to good research. You should read the best works and draw on them with a critical eye — sometimes agreeing, sometimes disagreeing. Learning to do that well is a major goal of higher education. It's one way you'll become a more thoughtful and informed person.

This is not the place to discuss how to write papers. My goal here is more limited. I simply want to say what it means to write papers honestly. That's really very simple. First, whenever you rely on the work of anyone else, cite it so your readers know. That's true whether you agree or disagree with the cited works. If you use anyone else's ideas, include a citation. If you use their exact words, use quotation marks *and* a citation.

Second, whenever you quote someone directly, use quotation marks. Longer quotes, running more than a few sentences, are indented rather than enclosed with quotation marks, but the principle is the same. Readers will understand this block indent is a quotation:

> Fourscore and seven years ago our fathers brought forth on this continent, a new nation, conceived in Liberty, and dedicated to the proposition that all men are created equal.
>
> Now we are engaged in a great civil war, testing whether that nation, or any nation so conceived and so dedicated, can long endure.[2]

No one will ever think you meant to plagiarize the Gettysburg Address. Still, you need to cite it. Citations are especially important when your sources are obscure or controversial. You must show readers exactly which sources you used, whether they're for data, analysis, or direct quotes.

---

2. Abraham Lincoln, Gettysburg Address, November 19, 1863, reprinted in Gary Wills, *Lincoln at Gettysburg: The Words that Remade America* (New York: Simon & Schuster, 1992), app. I:202–3 and app. III D 2:263.

To put it a little differently, your references (or their absence) shouldn't mislead readers. Use them to strengthen your analysis and amplify your ideas, never as a substitute for doing your own work.

One more important point about papers: you cannot hand in the same paper to more than one class. That's also true for homework assignments. If you write a paper on the Great Depression for an economics class, you can't turn it in to an American history class, too. You have to write another paper. You're not allowed to plagiarize your own work. You are still welcome to write about the Great Depression and even to rely on some of the same books and articles, but the paper itself should be substantially different. (If you *really* want to expand on an earlier paper, explain that to your current teacher and get approval. If you want to turn in the same paper to two current classes, talk to both teachers and get their approval.)

Tips on writing honest papers:

- Cite others' work whenever you rely on it.
- When you use someone's words, quote them accurately, mark them as a quotation, and include a citation.
- When you paraphrase, use your own distinctive voice, not a facsimile of the author's. Be sure to include a citation.
- Never represent anyone else's work as your own.
- Never hand in the same paper to two classes unless you have permission from both instructors.
- Never buy, sell, or "borrow" papers. Do your own work.

In the next chapter, I'll expand on how to write papers honestly. But these are the key ideas: do the work yourself, quote accurately, cite the work you use and the ideas you draw upon, and present all materials fairly.

Buying Papers on the Internet
Don't.

It's dishonest to buy (or sell!) papers. For that matter, it's dishonest to turn in papers you have lifted from friends, downloaded from the Internet, or cut-and-pasted from two or three sources. It doesn't matter whether your friends gave you permission or whether the information is freely available on the Web. It is dishonest to represent anyone else's work as your own. It's just as dishonest to provide your work to others.

This kind of cheating is often caught. Professors have seen lots of papers, and they have developed good antennae to pick up dishonest ones. There are usually telltale signs. Some papers just don't sound like a particular student. Others don't quite address the assignment. Occasionally, the introduction doesn't sound like the conclusion. For example, a paper might begin: "It's for sure America will sign to this international treaty." Then it might conclude, without quotation marks: "Having ratified this pact with such lofty ideals and soaring hopes, America will soon confront its harsh realities." The writer who fumbled through the first sentence could not have written the last one. Someone else did, and the student copied it. Still other papers include obvious signs of cheating such as antiquated citations or out-of-date references. "President Lincoln will probably defeat the Confederacy and win re-election." I'm betting he will. I just hope he doesn't go to the theater.

Faculty have also become more sophisticated about detecting fraud via the Internet. Although it's easy to cheat using the Web, it's easy to catch cheating the same way. Faculty simply select some text from a questionable student paper and do a Google search for it. They can also use computer services that now work with colleges to detect plagiarism and cheating. These services compare newly submitted student papers to everything in their databases, which include thousands of previously submitted student papers, all publicly available Web sites, and nearly all published articles. They automatically flag sentences in new papers matching those in the database. Then each newly submitted paper, honest or not, becomes part of this ever-expanding database.

This may sound like a cat-and-mouse game, but it's not. It's about honest work, personal integrity, and real learning. Buying papers is cheating. Colleges take it seriously with good reason. It's a direct assault on honest learning. Equally important, it's a self-inflicted wound on your own education.

USING THE INTERNET FOR RESEARCH

The Web has become integral to academic work. It's the fastest way to scan lots of sources, compare authors, gain access to specialized materials, and much more. It's a great research tool and an easy way to grab some quick facts. When did women get the vote in America? Does India have more people than China? How many miles, roughly, is the Indianapolis 500?

When you use the Internet, just remember a few basic points. One is that the quality of information varies widely. Anybody with a Web site or blog can say whatever they want. There's no quality control. If the *Encyclopaedia Britannica* Web site says D-day was June 6, 1944, you can count on it. If the *Encyclopedia Brittany* says it was April 1, 1984, check somewhere else. You need to use solid sources, and, even then, you may want to cross-check them. If you're unsure which sources to use, ask your professor or a reference librarian for guidance. They know the literature and can help.

Second, Web research allows you to zero in on a topic, but it sometimes strips away the context. The context may be essential, however, for you to understand the topic and explore its significance. If you search for "Iraq War + 2003," for instance, you'll get thousands of hits on the war itself, but you may not learn much about its setting in American politics or its implications throughout the Middle East. If that's important to you, you'll need to refocus your online search.

Third, it's soooo easy to drag-and-drop information from the Web into your computer. That's great for taking notes, but it can easily become great trouble. Since you already know the value of Internet research, let me mention a couple of potential problems so you can avoid them. One is that it's often easier to copy information than to read or understand it. (That's true of photocopying, too.) Another is that it invites cheating. Just drop a paragraph or two from someone's article into your paper. Unless you quote and cite it, however, you're plagiarizing. Finally, even if you are not trying to cheat, it's easy to lose track of what you copied and what you actually wrote yourself.

How should you handle these problems? First, you need to screen your sources of information. Some, like electronic journals, publish only high-quality articles, evaluated by professionals in their field. They reject papers that fall short of their standards. At the other extreme are Web sites run by the same people who write e-mails explaining that their father was a corrupt Nigerian millionaire and that they will generously share his fortune with you, if you would please send them your bank account and credit card numbers.

There are no gatekeepers online, no global editors to guarantee the quality of information. You have to judge it yourself. You have to determine which Web sites are reliable and which ones aren't.

Second, you need to decide if the wider context is important for understanding your topic. If it is, then you'll need to expand the scope of your research. On the Web, you'll probably want to search for additional text strings (for example, "Iraq war + polling" or "Iraq war + Saudi") and follow hyperlinks to background readings. To provide the political, social, and historical setting, you'll want to read significant articles and books. That's not always necessary, but for some issues it's crucial. To hit the bull's-eye, it helps to see the surrounding circles.

Third, don't drag-and-drop too much from the Web into your notes. It's hard to keep straight just who wrote what, and it invites trouble. When you do drag-and-drop some material, it's important to have a consistent system to mark someone else's words and ideas and where they came from. You need to identify the source page, first in your notes and later in your papers. Also, once you begin writing and drawing on your notes, you need a way to keep your words separate from those you've copied. In the next chapter, I'll describe a simple method for doing that — a way that works with quotations from books, articles, and electronic sources. Just put the letter Q at the beginning and end of any quoted materials. It works well because it's simple and stands out clearly in your notes. It's equally effective in your handwritten notes.

When you copy something from a Web site, be sure to copy the URL so you can cite it later. It's a good idea to write down the date you accessed it, too. Some citation styles require it, mainly because Internet content changes so often. If you use professional databases like Medline or MathSciNet, jot down the document ID number so you can add it to citations or easily return for more research.

Tips on Web research:
- Screen the quality of information you get off the Internet.
- Move beyond your targeted search and look for background materials to provide essential context. That means reading books and articles as well as Web content.
- Don't drag-and-drop too much into your notes. Summarize the information in your own words.
- Have a clear system, such as Q-quotes, to mark any material you drag-and-drop.
- Be sure to write down the URL of Web pages you use and the date you accessed them so you can cite them later. It's also a time-saver if you need to go back to the site. That's true for database identification numbers, too. Be sure to write them down.

LANGUAGE CLASSES

Learning a foreign language is one of the most common college experiences. Fortunately, it presents very few difficulties for doing honest work. The rules are straightforward and familiar. You can't copy homework or exams from anyone — from classmates, answer books, or published translations. You can't use computer-assisted translations, either. You know the basic principle: When you say you did the work yourself, you actually did it. That's as true for classes in Mandarin as it is for classes in Chinese art or history.

What about using a Chinese-English dictionary? Rules vary from teacher to teacher, and sometimes from assignment to assignment. You can generally use dictionaries for take-home work. They may help you learn new words and remind you of old ones. On the other hand, some teachers don't permit them for in-class quizzes and translations since they want you to master the vocabulary. One student passed along an important practical point, based on her classes in Arabic. Although she was allowed to use dictionaries for all her assignments, the translations in class "were generally timed, so thumbing through dictionaries was a disadvantage."[3] If you use dictionaries, then use them mainly as aides to learning vocabulary. You'll eventually need to know that anyway.

Beyond these basic issues, it's important to know how honest work actually helps you learn a foreign language.

"My goal," said one Italian professor, "is to help students become good listeners, good readers, and spontaneous speakers and writers." For classical languages, the goal is to read easily and translate accurately. Whatever the language, you'll master it only with practice. That means repeating oral exercises, listening to conversations, working on grammar and vocabulary, and writing translations. Homework exercises are designed to guide you along this path by immersing you in the language and gradually building on what you've already covered. Besides giving you practice, the exercises allow you to learn from your mistakes. "Mistakes are actually quite important," one professor told me. "Correcting them is how you learn the language."

---

3. Some students need more time for other important reasons. Some have learning disabilities, and others are still mastering English. If you need more time for an exam or an assignment, speak with your teacher *in advance* and explain your situation. You may be asked to provide a letter documenting your needs.

That's why it undercuts learning simply to copy the answers instead of working on the assignments. (It's obvious to teachers, too, according to everyone I spoke with.) To learn, you need to practice. It will give you an easy familiarity with what you already know and a chance to identify and correct mistakes. Remember that the goal is not simply to translate a few paragraphs correctly. The goal is to understand the language, to grasp the general rules of Spanish, Russian, or Japanese, and to learn how they apply to specific words and sentences.

Can you ever use published translations or answer keys? Yes, occasionally, if your teacher doesn't mind. But use them only to double-check your work or solve a sticky problem. "Don't use them until you've already wrestled with the problem yourself," one Latin professor explained. "Then, you can turn to a published translation to check your work or get past a rough spot." In other words, use prepared translations for self-guided teaching, not as substitutes for doing your own work.

Faculty in physics, chemistry, math, and economics told me exactly the same thing about answer books in their fields. As a way to check your work, they can serve as silent teachers. As a way to avoid work, they are dishonest and self-defeating.

> *Tip for all classes:* Don't use answer keys, published translations, or work by others as substitutes for doing your own work. You can use them occasionally, if your teacher approves, as guides to help you learn—to check your work, for example, or to overcome specific obstacles.

GROUP ASSIGNMENTS

While most class assignments are meant to be done individually, some are designed for small groups. Your professor may assemble these groups, or you may form your own. "I tell my students that this is an extremely efficient way to study," one scientist explained to me. "By looking for questions that will show up on the exam, students end up looking at the material differently. Three or four folks working together will put slightly different emphases on the information, and [they] may even have taken different notes."

When you work in small groups, it's important to know the professor's rules. They vary across classes and assignments, and that variation matters for doing honest work. Sometimes you are asked to study together but then to produce your own individual written work. Sometimes you are asked to produce a joint paper or group presentation. Sometimes you are simply encouraged to study together with no written assignment. It's important to know which one applies to your group and to your assignment. When in doubt, ask.

> *Tips on group assignments:* Know what the professor expects. What is to be done by the group, and what is to be done individually? If you are unsure, ask before doing the work. If one member of the group doesn't do his share, speak privately with the student first and then with the professor.

If the assignment is to study as a group and then turn in individual papers, it violates the rules to incorporate other students' work directly into yours. Talk with them, learn from them, but don't share their writing and don't copy their ideas word-for-word. "Shared writing like this will be obvious," one professor told me.

On the other hand, you may be asked to prepare a true group assignment, such as a class presentation. Encourage everyone in the group to pitch in and work honestly. When the group presents its work, give everyone credit. Working well in groups like this is rewarding in its own right. "It's good practice for the rest of [students'] lives," one scientist pointed out, "since so much of what we do is in collaboration with others." The downside is that you may also get some practice dealing with someone who doesn't pull a fair share of the load. If someone doesn't participate, or might be cheating, first speak privately with that student and then, if necessary, with the professor.

All this advice applies to group assignments. Of course, if the assignment is given to you individually, rather than as part of a group, you have to do it individually. That's true even if you study with a group. You can discuss the assignment with group members or other friends — in person, by e-mail, or in Internet chat rooms. It's fine to toss around ideas, but it's cheating to swap actual answers and submit them as your own. You have to write the assignment . . . by yourself, in your own words.

Problem Sets as Group Activities

The most common group task is to work together on problem sets. Teachers in math, economics, statistics, and the sciences encourage it, and for good reason. It's a great way to learn.

To avoid any suspicion of cheating, however, it's important to know your professor's rules about doing problem sets. What's perfectly fine for one teacher or one assignment may not be fine for another. You may be encouraged to write answers together, as a group. Or you may be explicitly told not to. There's nothing right or wrong about these varied assignments. They're just different, the same way open- and closed-book exams are different. Listen carefully to the rules governing each problem set, ask for clarification if you are unsure, and then respect the rules you are given.

There are really two issues here. One is avoiding dishonesty. If your name stands alone on a paper, it means you solved the problems yourself. You can consult others in the group — that's why it was formed — but you must do all the written work yourself. On the other hand, if you are listed as co-author of a group paper, then you participated in the joint work.

> *Tip on authorship:* If your name is alone on a paper, it means you did the work entirely yourself. If you are listed as a coauthor, you contributed to the group's work.

The other issue is how best to learn from group activity. This is not usually a question of cheating (although the lines are sometimes fuzzy), but it is important to your education. If there are four students in the group and four problem sets to do, the temptation is to divide the assignment. Even if your teacher permits the group to parcel out work this way, it still may not be the best way to learn. After all, you can't take exams that way, by passing the hard questions over to friends in the study group. That's why you need to learn how to think about the questions and solve the problems — all of them, not just 25 percent.

It's not enough just to "get the answers." That's why simply copying them cheats your own education. The goal of learning is not only finding answers but finding the best *paths* to answers. It's about the journey, as well as the destination. Problem sets are tools for finding these paths, or finding out if you've lost your way. It's a lot better to discover that on practice problems than on high-stakes exams.

That's why it's usually best if each group member does *all* the problem sets individually. Then you can go over some or all of them with the group, check each other's work, suggest corrections, and learn together. You'll know the material much better when it comes time to write papers and exams.

Tip on problem sets as group activities: When you do problem sets as a joint activity, each person should do the entire assignment individually and then go over it with the group. That's not a rule about honesty; it's a tip about how to learn.

What if you don't understand how some problems are solved? What if you're unsure about the right methods to use? Then it's fine to ask others to explain them, whether they're in your group or not. Before you ask for help, though, try to work out the solutions yourself. If you are still puzzled, go over the questions as often as you wish with friends, roommates, professors, tutors, TAs, and members of your study group. Focus on *how to solve problems*, rather than on the solutions themselves. Try to diagnose exactly where you are having difficulty. When you understand the right methods, you'll be able to solve the problems yourself. You'll be able to explain *why* you chose one technique or solution rather than another. In fact, that's a good test of whether you really understand the solution.

This advice applies to foreign languages as well as math, science, and economics. "Based on my own experience teaching introductory Latin," one professor explained, "it can sometimes be useful for students to consult each other on a particularly tough assignment or tough patch." But don't consult others, he said, "until you've already tackled the problem yourself." If the help you receive is extensive or crucial, he suggested acknowledging it in the written assignment. That's not required, but it's a good idea for a couple of reasons. It eliminates any confusion about who did what work and, just as important, it lets your teacher know exactly which issues are troublesome and need more instruction. If they are hard for you, they are probably hard for your classmates, too.

As you learn together, don't cross the line and copy down answers directly from someone else and hand them in as your own work (unless you are specifically allowed to coauthor assignments and include others' names on the paper). The same standards apply to copying from answer books or old problem sets. If your name stands alone on the paper, then you must write all the answers yourself, in your own words. Discuss. Contribute. Learn from friends or your study group. Feel free to ask for help again and again. Then do your own work. That's the best way to learn.

Tips on how to set up an effective study group of your own: You can learn a lot if you study with the right people in the right setting. With the wrong people in a noisy place, though, you'll simply waste time. Here are some tips, based on conversations with experienced undergraduates:

- Study with one to three other students. Larger groups spend too much time chatting. That's fun, but it's not studying.
- Work together in a quiet place, where you can talk without bothering others. The library may have some rooms for study groups. Or there may be a coffee shop near campus that's not too crowded. Do not study together in a dorm room; there are too many distractions. (Speaking of distractions, shut off your cell phone.)
- Set a specific time to begin and end the session. Make sure everybody knows you will begin on time. Most sessions last about sixty to ninety minutes, perhaps a little longer when you are studying for finals. Setting a time to end the session will push you to work efficiently.
- Pick specific topics in advance to discuss and make sure everybody studies the same thing beforehand. Do not parcel out the work you'll discuss, with some people studying one thing and some another. Hypothetically, that seems efficient. In practice, it doesn't work. If there is a study guide, decide in advance which part you'll discuss. If there are ten assigned problems and you only want to discuss half, make sure everybody does the same odd (or even) ones.
- Select people you'll enjoy working with.
  - They should be at about your academic level, so you can keep up with them, and they can keep up with you. That way, you can teach each other, and it won't be a one-way street.
  - Choose people who want to work and will contribute to the group. Avoid those who don't study for class and just want a free ride. Again, you want a two-way street for mutual teaching and learning.

How do you select the right study partners? One student told me his approach. "I try to pick other students who always come to class and show up on time instead of fifteen minutes late. I like those who say something valuable in class instead of just trying to impress the teacher. They'll have something to say in the study group, too." Excellent advice.

At the Blackboard with Your Study Group

The most inviting time to copy answers is when everyone works together at the blackboard. After one student solves a physics or engineering problem, it's easy for everyone else to scribble down the answer. "Most teachers consider this cheating," the head of one math program told me, "and we can easily spot identical work like this."

There's a better approach and a more honest one, she explained. Work through the problems — individually and collectively — and make sure everyone understands them. Then *erase the solutions on the blackboard* and let everyone do the work individually. Reworking the solutions for yourself is not useless "make work." It's useful practice and genuine learning.

That's true even if the person writing answers on the blackboard is the teaching assistant for your section. It's not cheating to copy the TA's answers. After all, they are written out for the whole class. But you won't learn much by rote copying. The goal is to understand the process and master the technique, not repeat the answers mechanically. If the TA skips over these key elements or if you still don't understand, be sure to ask.

Final Thoughts on Group Learning

One scientist summarized his advice on group work like this, "I generally want the students to figure out *how* to solve the problem together. The actual solution should be done individually. The point [of solving problems individually] is to give each student practice with skills that can only be acquired by doing them." To see if you've actually acquired these skills, try to defend your answer to the group or even to yourself. *Why* is this answer the right one? *How* exactly did you reach it? Be sure you can answer these questions.

Time and again, teachers mentioned the importance of participating actively in group sessions. "You can't really learn in groups if you're passive," one physicist told me. "After all, it's not about getting the answers to specific questions. It's really about understanding the process, learning how to answer hard questions." You can learn that in groups, but only if you join in. First, work together to master the process; then solve the problems yourself. If you're still stumped, ask for help. Then try again — on your own.

That's probably the best approach even if your teacher permits joint written work. Students who simply copy the answers might not understand them. *Their learning gaps will show up later on exams, papers, and more advanced work.*

Tips on how to use study groups:
- Be active, not passive, in study groups.
- Learn how to answer questions and how to think about problems, rather than what the specific answers are. Once you truly understand the process, you'll be able to answer the questions yourself—on homework, papers, and exams—and you'll be able to defend the answers you've got.

That's also why published answer manuals can impede learning. They're easy to buy and provide ready solutions to problem sets in major textbooks. Some teachers think it's okay to use them; others don't. In any case, it's not a good idea to lean too heavily on them. As a quick way to check your answers, they can be a useful source of feedback. As a substitute for doing the work, they short-circuit your education. Just remember how we all learned to ride bicycles. Eventually, the training wheels had to come off.

These manuals also raise the crucial issue of honest work. If you copy the answers from a book, you're cheating. It's the same as copying answers from another student or downloading them from the Web. It's simply not your own work.

Tips on honesty in group assignments: In some classes, you work with study groups but are expected to complete assignments individually (rather than hand in joint projects). It's vital to know what you can and cannot do together. A few pointers:
- Know your professor's expectations for group work *before you hand in your work*. What should the group do together and what should be done individually?
- It's fine for the group to discuss problem sets, class topics, and so forth. It's fine to ask others to explain methods and solutions you don't understand. Together, you can go over the problems several times until you understand.
- But it's cheating for others to provide answers to you—on paper, on the blackboard, or in a printed answer manual—and for you to copy them and turn them in as your own individual work. It's also a terrible way to learn and will come back to bite you on exams and more advanced work.

Once you understand the material, you should write your own answers, in your own words.

LABS

The most common group assignments, aside from problem sets, are science labs. Together with your lab partner, you calibrate instruments, perform experiments, collect data, clean up explosions, and call the fire department. Better yet, you can follow safety procedures. After doing all this activity together, however, you should write your lab reports separately and reach your own conclusions.

The rules here are straightforward. Do the lab experiments jointly (if that's the assignment), but keep your own personal lab notes and write your own reports. *Never* borrow data or written work without your professor's explicit permission.

> *Tip on working with lab partners:* It's fine to do lab work together with your partners, but you should keep your own lab notes and write up the results individually.

Accurate Lab Notes

Whenever you do lab work, keep accurate records of both your procedures and results. Different laboratories do this in different ways. Some use traditional lab notebooks; others use computers; and still others use questionnaires designed for specific experiments. Whichever method you use, write down the results as soon as possible. Don't trust your memory. Don't fudge the results. And don't use anyone else's data without your teacher's permission.

Teachers *do* sometimes give permission to use others' data. If an experiment misfires, for example, your instructor may give you other results to evaluate. Or she may provide some data to the entire class. The reason is simple: labs are designed to teach you how to analyze data as well as how to conduct experiments. But unless your instructor allows you to use other data, stick with your own.

Traditionally, scientists record their results in special notebooks — bound volumes with numbered pages — which are tailor-made for the purpose. It's hard to cover up mistakes using lab books like this. That's the point. "Never use Wite-Out or rip pages from a lab notebook," one chemistry professor told me. "That's one reason the notebooks have numbered pages. If you make an error, cross it out neatly and continue documenting your observations and results."

Why should you save your mistakes? "Because your observations and procedures are just as important as your results," one scientist emphasized to me. "If you record your procedures and results accurately, your teachers can help you figure out the problems, if there are any." That's exactly what math and physics professors say about showing your work. It shows them how you think about a problem. If any difficulties crop up, it helps you pin them down.

Tips on lab records:
- Check with your instructor (or head of your lab) about record keeping. You may be asked to use lab notebooks, computers, or packets designed for specific experiments.
- Enter data as soon as possible after an experiment. Don't rely on your memory.
- Record even your experimental mistakes. Later, after performing the experiment correctly, neatly cross out the errors in your lab notebook. Don't rip out pages or use correction fluid. The original data should still be readable. If you record data on computers instead of notebooks, label the old data "incorrect" (or use a strike-through font) but don't wipe it out. With some help from your instructors, you may be able to learn from these mistakes.

Today, many labs have replaced notebooks with computers, equipped with software for data analysis. The technologies may change, but the rules for entering data remain the same.

- Do it as soon as possible after the experiment.
- Record your results accurately, even if the experiment failed.
- When you repeat an experiment, don't erase the old data. Label it as "incorrect," but keep it so you can check what went wrong, or perhaps discover it was okay after all.
- Use only your own data, unless you are explicitly told otherwise.

Then write up the conclusions on your own.

Honest Data
The crux of honest lab work is the truthful presentation of experimental data. Your lab notebook and computer records should be honest, com-

plete, and reliable, showing exactly how you did experiments and what results you obtained, even if they weren't up to expectations.

Never make up lab results, borrow them from others, or bend the results
to fit your needs. Don't modify the results arbitrarily. Don't draw perfect
graphs and fill in the observations later.

The National Science Foundation calls such violations "scientific misconduct." Misconduct, it says, means "fabrication, falsification, plagiarism,
or other serious deviations from accepted practices in preparing, carrying
out, or reporting results" from scientific activities.[4] You may not be working on an NSF grant, but the same sensible rules apply.

There are temptations, of course. Sometimes, you are running late and
could finish quickly if you invented some numbers or "borrowed" them
from a friend. Sometimes, your experimental results don't match the expected numbers. Again, it's tempting to insert the "right" numbers rather
than figure out exactly what went wrong. Were the measurements off? Was
the equipment calibrated incorrectly? Did you make a simple mistake in the
experiment? Everybody makes mistakes. One way to learn how science is
practiced is to review the proper procedures and compare them with what
you actually did.

The most common lab mistakes, one biologist told me, come before the
experiments begin. Students sometimes fail to read the instructions carefully or forget to line up all the equipment and materials. If you're missing
a chemical or beaker in the midst of an experiment, it may be too late to re-
cover. You'll learn much more by using orderly procedures, and you'll gen-
erate much better data to work with.

> *Tip:* Before beginning any experiment, read the instructions carefully and
> assemble all the equipment and materials you need. Also, be prepared to
> record your data.

When you're finished, your instructor or lab supervisor might ask to see
your records. That's perfectly appropriate. In introductory courses, it's to teach
you the best methods. In more advanced work, it's to evaluate your research
progress, improve collaboration, and ensure integrity throughout the lab.

---

4. *Federal Register* 56 (May 14, 1991): 22286–90.

Honest data is the foundation of lab integrity, and it is expected from everyone, from undergraduates to professors. Violations are treated seriously at all levels. A physicist at Bell Labs, one of the world's leading research facilities, was recently fired for fabricating results in nanoelectronics and superconductivity. Another physicist was dismissed from Berkeley's Lawrence Livermore National Laboratory when his celebrated discovery of elements 116 and 118 proved fraudulent.[5] The investigations began when other scientists could not repeat his experimental results.

It's not just scientists who must present honest, complete data. Everyone should, just as they should present reliable quotes and citations. A prize-winning book on early American gun ownership raised questions when no one else could locate many key documents on which it was allegedly based.[6] Outside experts investigated and sustained the most serious charges of misconduct. The professor was dismissed.

Not only must you present honest data; you must present it fairly. You can't leave out the bad news. Let's say you are testing a hypothesis and some of your experimental results don't support it. It's perfectly fine to double-check the experiment, see if you made a mistake, and try again. All that should be recorded faithfully in your lab notes. But once you have completed the reevaluation and fixed any problems, you should present the results fully and candidly, whether they agree with your hypothesis or not.

Tips on honest lab work:
- Lab partners may work together on experiments and discuss their work, but they are always required to keep their own notebooks and write up the results individually, without assistance.
- Never copy or make up data on experiments.
- Don't omit or hide unfavorable results. Record them in your lab notes.
- Present your experimental results honestly, even if you know they are "wrong" and even if they contradict your hypothesis.

---

5. Robert L. Park, "The Lost Innocence of Physics," *Times Education Supplement* (London), July 24, 2002.

6. Michael A. Bellesiles, *Arming America: The Origins of a National Gun Culture* (New York: Alfred A. Knopf, 2000). Bellesiles was both professor of history and director of Emory University's Center for the Study of Violence.

The same is true in history, sociology, political science, economics . . . in every field. One of the most damning findings about the book on gun ownership was its "egregious misrepresentation" of historical data. Outside experts found the author simply excluded some findings that disagreed with his.[7]

Whatever your subject, it violates basic research ethics to leave out unfavorable results. It's tempting to omit them from your papers or presentations, but you shouldn't. Remember, this is not a court case or debating contest where you present only selected facts, chosen to help your side. Your aim should be to present the results honestly and completely, warts and all. That's how good scholarship moves forward. Using this data, you may come up with a better hypothesis or more powerful interpretation. Or maybe someone else will. In any case, you should present your results fully and accurately.

CLASS PARTICIPATION

In many classes, especially seminars, part of your grade depends on class participation. Teachers *love* active, engaged discussions, where students raise useful questions, listen carefully to each other, and make thoughtful points, based on the readings. There's no more rewarding way to teach . . . or learn.

Honesty is not an issue in class discussions, but students do have legitimate questions about what counts as "participation" and what grade they should receive for it. Some questions are inevitable since judgments about participation are subjective. Others arise because teachers rarely specify what counts as participation.

---

7. When Bellesiles's critics could not find some crucial documents he had cited, they cried foul. Emory appointed an outside committee of eminent historians to investigate. They reached a number of damning conclusions and used the term "egregious misrepresentation," quoted above. "No one," they said, "has been able to replicate Professor Bellesiles' results [of low percentage of guns] for the places or dates he lists." They also found he had excluded data that contradicted his findings, notably Alice Hanson Jones's higher figures on gun ownership. They concluded that Bellesiles's "scholarly integrity is seriously in question." The report, made on July 10, 2002, is available at http://www.emory.edu/central/NEWS/Releases/Final_Report.pdf. Bellesiles's response is at http://www.emory.edu/central/NEWS/Releases/B_statement.pdf.

There is no way to avoid subjective judgments, but it's easy to say what counts as effective participation. Most teachers agree on three main elements:

- Do you attend class regularly?
- Have you done the assigned work so your comments and questions are solidly based?
- Do your contributions advance the class discussion?

You can contribute in lots of ways — by raising questions, offering answers, or playing off other student comments. To do that effectively, though, you need to keep pace with the assignments and listen respectfully to your classmates as well as your teacher. That way, you can respond to each other and to the material, a fruitful give-and-take from which everyone can learn.

Keep in mind that a seminar is *not* a lecture, where you sit quietly, take notes, and perhaps ask a question or two. A seminar (or weekly discussion section for a lecture course) is a guided dialogue, based on assigned work. You won't get the most out of it if you sit mute, talk over others, or arrive without preparing. "Passive learning is not the way we do things," one seminar leader told me. "It is expected that a student plays an active part in learning."

To play that active part, you need to do the readings beforehand. Your goal should be to engage the material fully — to grapple with it — first when you read it and later when you discuss it in class.

Don't worry about "showing the teacher what you know." Papers and exams give you plenty of opportunity to do that. Don't worry about agreeing with everyone else. It's perfectly fine to take a different perspective, as long as you keep an open mind, respect others' opinions, and offer reasons for your views. As one professor put it, "Dialogue and debate are fundamental norms of our system of higher education."

It's also fine to try out new ideas, new angles on the subject, even if you're not completely sure what you think about them. Consider it a "test drive" for your ideas. You have my permission (and your teachers'!) to probe your own thinking in these group discussions. Just make sure you have done the readings and homework first.

The focus should be on joining the conversation, exploring the material, and discussing it openly with your classmates. That fosters a more lively seminar and a richer learning experience. In the process, it reveals how you approach the subject and what you think about it.

Tips on how to participate profitably in class discussions:
- Attend regularly and arrive on time.
- Keep up with the assigned work.
- Listen to your fellow students as well as your teacher.
- Advance the discussion with your own questions, answers, and responses to others' comments.

One final point: try to say something during the first or second class session. Make an effort to break the ice early. Don't wait silently, hoping you'll find the perfect moment to say the perfect thing. Class discussions don't work that way. They are not about making perfect comments. They're about learning through give-and-take, through questions and answers, including mistakes and missteps. Believe me, we all make them. If you don't speak during the first few sessions, you can easily slip into the routine of never participating. There's a simple solution: pitch in early, even if it's just a small comment or question. Once you've joined the conversation, you'll feel more comfortable participating again.

Your teacher wants exactly the same thing: to get the discussion rolling, with lots of students contributing. One experienced professor told me he "might begin by calling on students and asking them to share their thoughts on a reading or on another student's previous comment. Students should not feel as though they are being picked on. [My goal] is not to 'test' or 'intimidate' students," but to foster discussion and encourage students to "feel confident sharing their ideas with their classmates and teacher."

If you are shy or simply uncomfortable about speaking in class, you may need to push yourself a little. If you're nervous about speaking off the cuff, jot down an idea or two from the readings and use them to ask a question or make a comment in class. If you are uncomfortable speaking in groups, drop by the professor's office hours and begin a conversation there. After a

Tip on class participation: Try to say something during the first session or two, even if it's only a small comment. It will open the door to more participation later.

Another tip: Sit at the table in seminars and discussion sections. Slouching in the back row, behind everyone else, invites passive listening instead of active participation.

one-on-one discussion, you may feel better about participating in class. You can also get some help from your college learning skills center. It deals with these issues all the time and will have lots of useful suggestions.

APPEALING A LOW GRADE

Sometimes, when your professor hands back lab reports, papers, or exams, you think your grade is too low. As you hear the answers explained, you realize yours was correct and you weren't given full credit. My advice: give yourself some time to calm down, mull it over, and review your answer. Maybe, on second look, it's not quite the Nobel Prize winner you remembered.

If you still think you deserve additional credit, it's perfectly fine to discuss it with your professor and appeal the grade. But don't do that until you have reread the exam and settled on specific reasons for your appeal. "I really need a better grade" is *not* a reason.

A little courtesy helps, too. Keep the discussion positive and concrete. Snarling about incompetent grading will only make your teacher grumpy. Generally speaking, you should avoid all phrases that include the word "moron." Instead, you might say, "I think my answer is very close to what you mentioned in your last lecture, and I'd really appreciate your taking another look." Or, "You said the answer should cover three main points, and I think mine did." And it's always fine to ask, "How could I do better?"

Your professor undoubtedly has some standard procedures for regrading, and you should ask about them. Your grade might be raised. Even if it isn't, you might learn what you did wrong so you can do better next time. That's valuable, too, because there will be many "next times," in many other classes.

One common problem, especially in math, statistics, and some sciences, is failing to show all your work. It's not enough simply to write down the answer, even if it's correct. You won't get full credit if you don't show full work. That's partly to prevent cheating, but there are other reasons, too. It also allows the professor to give you partial credit for what you got right. If you got the answer wrong, it allows the professor to identify the problem and show you how to correct it.

By showing your work, you're showing how you think through a problem. That's exactly what teachers want to know. "Just writing down an answer merits no (or almost no) credit at all," one physicist told me. "We're trying to teach students how to approach problems: how to set them up, how to carry through the calculations, and how to interpret the final results. In other words, how to think physically. . . . *If a student does not show his work, he is leaving out the very thing I'm trying to assess."*

So, follow the advice you've heard from every math teacher since third grade: show your work.

Finally, if you appeal your grades, you must follow one hard-and-fast rule. You cannot modify your work in any way before regrading. That's cheating.

> *Tips on appealing low grades:*
> • Reread your answer before deciding whether to appeal.
> • Courteously explain the specific reasons for your appeal.
> • Never change anything on the exam before regrading.

HONOR CODES

Some schools use honor codes to ensure academic integrity. Students typically sign a pledge to do honest work, monitor each other, and report violations. They are not only responsible for doing honest work themselves; they must report cheating by others. They also promise to behave responsibly outside class and play a major role in judging infractions.

Problems are usually dealt with by honors councils, rather than college deans. Some councils are run entirely by students; others include faculty and administrators. In either case, students play a critical role in making honor codes work, mostly by taking responsibility for academic honesty and by emphasizing its central place in education.

The actual content of honest work and responsible behavior is no different from that of other schools. Students pledge to do their own work, not to plagiarize, cheat, or purchase papers, and to follow their professors' rules for papers, lab reports, and exams. Outside class, they pledge not to harass, intimidate, or threaten others — the same rules that apply in most universities, whether or not they use honor codes.

What is different is the responsibility students take upon themselves, individually and collectively, for maintaining and promoting these high ethical standards. "Students should constantly evaluate their own actions, inside or outside of the classroom," one student told me. "This covers everything from day-to-day interactions between students to academic honesty to the manner in which the [college] Senate allocates student body funds."

Professors rely on students living up to these standards, and students count on each other. Faculty don't monitor in-class exams, for instance, and often allow students to take closed-book exams in the college library or their dorm rooms. They are confident students will adhere to the rules. Everyone knows that widespread violations would sabotage the whole system.

The purpose of honor codes goes well beyond catching dishonesty or even discouraging it by monitoring and punishment. As one student put it, "The feeling of being watched runs completely counter to the point of the [honor code], as it leaves people feeling infantilized and mistrusted. The benefit of the [honor code] is that students can feel secure in making their own ethical choices because they know that they will be treated like adults, that is, rationally, with compassion and understanding."

I heard that again and again from students. *The most profound goal of the honor system, they said, was a positive one: to create an ethos of honesty and responsibility in academic and social life.*

These codes are more common in teaching colleges than in large universities. That's no surprise. They work best where students know each other well and have a strong sense of community. Indeed, the codes usually become central pillars of that community, vital elements in the school's self-definition. They encourage a student culture of fairness and integrity, promote individual and collective responsibility, and foster strong bonds of trust between students and faculty.

These are goals well worth aspiring to, whether or not your school uses an honor code.

3

PLAGIARISM AND
ACADEMIC HONESTY

· · · · · · · · · · · · · ·

The last chapter included some basic ideas about writing papers honestly. In this chapter, I'll expand on them and show you how to avoid problems.

The biggest problem is misrepresenting someone else's work as your own. That's plagiarism, and it's a serious breach of academic rules, whether it's borrowed words, proofs, data, drawings, or ideas. When it's caught — and it often is — it leads to severe consequences, anything from failing a paper to failing a course. In extreme cases, it leads to suspension or expulsion. It's not a parking ticket. It's a highway crash. If it looks deliberate, it's a highway crash without seat belts.

Plagiarism is rare, but it does happen occasionally. The reason is sometimes a simple, innocent mistake. If book notes are garbled, a student may be unable to separate another author's words from his own. Later, when those notes are used for writing a paper, he might inadvertently treat the other author's words as his own original language. Even if it's an accident, it's no fun trying to prove that to a skeptical professor or dean.

Fortunately, this problem is easily prevented. I'll show you a few simple techniques, beginning with Q-quotes, to keep your notes straight. Using them, you can tell exactly what you wrote and what someone else did. Problem solved.

Of course, bad notes are not the only reason for plagiarism. Students rushing to finish a paper may forget to include the necessary citations. Some students are just sloppy, and others don't understand the citation rules. Sadly, a few cheat deliberately.[1]

---

1. It is always wrong to use others' work without proper attribution. The most troubling cases involve intentional use of another author's work without full attribution. That is the classic definition of plagiarism. Some use a wider definition, which includes

Whatever the cause, plagiarism is a serious violation of academic rules — for undergraduates, graduate students, and faculty. Misrepresenting someone else's words or ideas as your own constitutes fraud. Remember the basic principles of academic integrity: When you say you did the work yourself, you actually did it. When you rely on someone else's work, you cite it. When you use someone else's words, you quote them openly and accurately. When you present research materials, you present them fairly and truthfully. Quotations, data, lab experiments, and the ideas of others should never be falsified or distorted.

CITE OTHERS' WORK TO AVOID PLAGIARISM

Citation rules follow from these basic principles of openness and honesty. If the words are someone else's, they must be clearly marked as quotations, either by quotation marks or block indentation, followed by a citation. It's not enough merely to mention an author's name. If it's a direct quote, use quotation marks and a full citation. If it's a paraphrase of someone else's words, use your own language, not a close imitation of the work being cited, and include a proper reference.

The same rules apply to visual images, architectural drawings, databases, graphs, statistical tables, spoken words, and information taken from the Internet. If you use someone else's work, cite it. Cite it even if you think the work is wrong and you intend to criticize it. Cite it even if the work is freely available in the public domain. Cite it even if the author gave you permission to use the work. All these rules follow from the same idea: acknowledge what you take from others. The only exception is when you rely on commonly known information. When you discuss gravity, you don't need to footnote Isaac Newton.

The penalties for violating these rules are serious. For students, they can lead to failed courses and even expulsion. For faculty, they can lead to demotion or even loss of tenure. The penalties are severe because academic honesty is central to the university.

---

unintentional copying and borrowing. I call that "accidental plagiarism." Even if it's accidental borrowing—the spoiled fruits of sloppy notes rather than deliberate theft—it is still a serious problem. Whether or not you call it plagiarism, it's a major breach of academic rules.

Tips on avoiding plagiarism: When in doubt, give credit by citing the original source.
- If you use an author's exact words, enclose them in quotation marks and include a citation.
- If you paraphrase another author, use your own language. Don't imitate the original. Be sure to include a citation.
- If you rely on or report someone else's ideas, credit their source, whether you agree with them or not.

TAKING NOTES WITH Q-QUOTES

Some honest writers find themselves in hot water, accused of plagiarism, because their notes are so bad they cannot not tell what they copied and what they wrote themselves. You can avoid that by clearly distinguishing your words from others'.

All you need is a simple way to identify quotes and keep them separate from your own words and ideas.

The common solution — using ordinary quotation marks in your notes — doesn't actually work so well in practice. For one thing, quotation marks are small, so it's easy to overlook them later when you return to your notes to write a paper. Second, they don't tell you which page the quote comes from, something you need to know for proper citations. Third, if there's a quote within a quote, it's hard to keep your markings straight.

There's a better way. To avoid all this confusion, simply use the letter Q and the page number to begin all quotations in your notes. To end the quote, write Q again. It's painless, and it's easy to spot the Q's when you read your notes and write your papers.

Begin your notes for each new item by writing down the author, title, and other essential data. (The exact information you need is described in part 2, in the citation chapters.) You'll need this information for each book, article, and Web site you use. With this publication data plus Q-quotes, you'll

Tip on using Q-quotes to identify exact words:
Q157 Churchill's eloquence rallied the nation during the worst days of the war.Q

be able to cite effectively from your own notes, without having to return to the original publication.

This system is simple, clear, and effective. It works equally well for typed and handwritten notes. It easily handles quotes within quotes. Looking at your notes, you'll know exactly which words are the author's, and which page they are on. You'll know if he is quoting anyone else. And you'll know that anything *outside* the Q-quotes is your own paraphrase.

> *Tip on paraphrasing:* Make sure your paraphrase does not closely resemble the author's words. When in doubt, double-check your wording against the original.

Because quotes can be complicated, let's see how these Q-quotes work in more detail. First, some quotes begin on one page and end on another. To show where the page break falls, insert a double slash (//) inside the quote. (A double slash stands out, just as Q does.) That way, if you use only part of the quote, you can cite the correct page without having to chase down the original again. To illustrate:

> Q324–25 Mark Twain's most important works deal with his boyhood on the river. He remembered // that distant time with great affection. He returned to it again and again for inspiration.Q

The first sentence is on page 324; the next one is on both pages; the third is only on page 325. Using Q-quotes with a double slash gives you all this information quickly and easily.

Quotes can be complicated in other ways, too. You may wish to cut out some needless words or add a few to make the quote understandable. Fortunately, there are straightforward rules to handle both changes.

SHORTENING QUOTATIONS WITH ELLIPSES . . .

Although quotes need to be exact, you are allowed to shorten them if you follow two rules. First, your cuts cannot change the quote's meaning. Second, you must show the reader exactly where you omitted any words. That's done with an ellipsis, which is simply three dots . . . with spaces before and after each one.

If the omitted words come in the middle of a sentence, an ellipsis is all you need.

Original   I walked downtown, which took at least thirty minutes, and saw her.

Shortened   I walked downtown . . . and saw her.

If the two parts of your quote come from two separate sentences, use an ellipsis plus a period (that is, three dots plus a period) to separate the two parts.

Original   I walked downtown. After walking more than thirty minutes, I rounded the corner and saw her.

Shortened 1   I walked downtown. . . . and saw her.

Shortened 2   I walked . . . . more than thirty minutes.

Explanation   Both shortened sentences use three ellipses plus a period. In the first, the period comes immediately after the word "downtown," because that's where the period falls in the original sentence. In the second, there is a space before the period because the original sentence continues.

Because ellipses are sometimes confusing, it may help to go over them again. Remember that they have a simple purpose: to signal deliberate omissions from any text you quote. These omissions can come in three places, and each is handled slightly differently.

	LOCATION OF OMISSION	HOW YOU SIGNAL THE OMISSION
A	In the middle of a single sentence	Simple ellipsis
B	Immediately after the end of a sentence	Period in its normal place, followed by an ellipsis
C	Starting in the middle of a sentence, ending at the conclusion of that sentence or later	Ellipsis, followed by a period

Now let me illustrate A, B, and C, using a simple example.

Example: Granted, this example is easy and simple. Perhaps it is silly. But I hope it is clear and useful.

	LOCATION OF OMISSION	ILLUSTRATION
A	In the middle of a single sentence	Granted, this example is . . . simple.
B	Immediately after the end of a sentence	Granted, this example is easy and simple. . . . But I hope it is clear and useful.
C	Starting in the middle of a sentence, ending at the conclusion of that sentence or later.	Granted, this example is easy . . . . But I hope it is clear and useful.

Omissions like these are perfectly acceptable as long as you signal them (with ellipses) and you don't change the quoted author's meaning.

ADDING WORDS [IN BRACKETS] TO CLARIFY A QUOTE

Occasionally, you need to add a word or two to clarify a quote. Perhaps the original sentence uses a pronoun instead of a person's name. For clarity, you might wish to include the name. Again, you cannot change the quote's meaning, and you need to signal the reader that you are modifying it slightly. You do that by using [brackets] to show exactly what you have inserted. Consider this original text:

Original text   Q237 Condoleezza Rice, President Bush's closest advisor, was speaking in New York that day. The President called and asked her to return to Washington immediately.Q

Now, let's say you want to quote only the second sentence. An exact quote wouldn't make much sense since the reader won't know whom the president was summoning. To correct that, you need to add a few words and bracket them to make it clear that you've added them to the original:

Your quote with brackets
"The President called and asked [his National Security Advisor Condoleezza Rice] to return to Washington immediately."

That's an accurate quote even though you added several bracketed words. If you added the same words without brackets, however, it would be a misquotation.

One important rule: These additions [with brackets] and omissions (with ellipses . . .) should not change the quote's meaning in any way. The statement belongs to another writer, not to you. You're welcome to praise it or to damn it, but not to twist it.

QUOTES WITHIN QUOTES

The phrase you are quoting may itself contain a quotation. One advantage of using Q-quotes for your notes is that you can simply put quotation marks wherever they appear in the text. For example: Q47 He yelled, "Come here, quick," and I ran over.Q Since you are using Q's to mark off the entire quote, there will be no confusion later when you write a paper with these notes.

USING Q-QUOTES TO HANDLE COMPLICATED QUOTATIONS

Now that we've covered the basics of Q-quotes plus ellipses, brackets, and quotes within quotes, you are equipped to handle even the most complex quotes, first in your notes and then in your papers. To illustrate that, let's combine all these elements in one example:

> Q157–58 Some of Churchill's most famous speeches // were actually recorded by professional actors imitating his distinctive voice and cadence. . . . The recordings were so good that [one friend] said, "I knew Winston well and still can't tell who is speaking."Q

This notation makes it clear that

- the first few words appear on page 157 and the rest are on page 158;
- some words from the original are omitted after the word "cadence";
- there is a period after "cadence" and then three dots, indicating that the first sentence ended at the word "cadence" and that the omission came after that;
- the bracketed words "one friend" are not in the original text; and
- the final words are actually a quotation from someone else. They are included as a quote by the author you are citing.

With clear notation like this, you will be able to cite portions of this complicated quote later, without returning to the original article and with no chance of accidental plagiarism. It's not difficult. Actually, it takes more time to explain it than to use it!

USING THE INTERNET WITHOUT PLAGIARIZING

You need to be especially alert to these citation issues when you use the Web. Internet research is very efficient, especially when you don't need to read long stretches of text. You can do extensive targeted searches, quickly check out multiple sources, access sophisticated databases, click on article summaries or key sentences, and then drag-and-drop material into your notes. That's all perfectly fine. In fact, it's often the best way to conduct research. But it's also crucial to be a good bookkeeper. You need to use a simple, consistent method to keep straight what some author said and what you paraphrased.

The easiest way is to stick with the method you use for printed books and articles: *put Q-quotes around everything you drag-and-drop from electronic sources.* You can supplement that, if you wish, by coloring the author's text red or blue, or by using a different font. Just be consistent. That way you won't be confused in three or four weeks, when you are reviewing your notes and writing your paper.

One more thing: be sure to write down the Web site's address so you can cite it or return to it for more research. Just copy the URL into your notes. It's probably a good idea to include the date you accessed it, too. Some citation styles ask for it. If the item appears in a database and has a document identification number, copy that, too.

QUOTING AND PARAPHRASING WITHOUT PLAGIARIZING: A TABLE OF EXAMPLES

A simple example can illustrate how to quote and paraphrase properly, and how to avoid some common mistakes. The following table shows the main rules for citation and academic honesty, using a sentence written by "Jay Scrivener" about Joe Blow. I'll use footnote 99 to show when that sentence is cited.

QUOTING WITHOUT PLAGIARIZING

Joe Blow was a happy man, who often walked down the road whistling and singing.	Sentence in the book *Joe Blow: His Life and Times,* by Jay Scrivener

WHAT'S RIGHT

"Joe Blow was a happy man, who often walked down the road whistling and singing."[99]	**Correct:** Full quote is inside quotation marks, followed by citation to *Joe Blow: His Life and Times*.
According to Scrivener, Blow "often walked down the road whistling and singing."[99] "Joe Blow was a happy man," writes Scrivener.[99]	**Correct:** Each partial quote is inside quote marks, followed by a citation. The partial quotes are not misleading.
According to Scrivener, Blow was "a happy man," who often showed it by singing tunes to himself.[99]	**Correct:** Partial quote is inside quotation marks; nonquoted materials are outside. The paraphrase (about singing tunes to himself) accurately conveys the original author's meaning without mimicking his actual words. Citation properly follows the sentence.
Joe Blow seemed like "a happy man," the kind who enjoyed "whistling and singing."[99]	**Correct:** Two partial quotes are each inside quotation marks; nonquoted materials are outside. Citation properly follows sentence.
Joe appeared happy and enjoyed whistling and singing to himself.[99]	**Correct:** This paraphrase is fine. It's not too close to Scrivener's original wording. The citation acknowledges the source.

WHAT'S WRONG

| Joe Blow was a happy man, who often walked down the road whistling and singing. (no citation) | **Wrong:** It is plagiarism to quote an author's exact words or to paraphrase them closely without *both* quotation marks and proper citation. Acknowledge your sources! |

Joe Blow was a happy man, who often walked down the road whistling and singing.[99]	**Wrong:** These are actually Scrivener's exact words. It is plagiarism to use them without indicating explicitly that it is a quote. It is essential to use quotation marks (or block indentation for longer quotes), *even if* you give accurate citation to the author. So, this example is wrong because it doesn't use quotation marks, even though it cites the source.
Joe Blow was a happy man and often walked down the road singing and whistling. (no citation)	**Wrong:** Although the words are not exactly the author's, they are *very similar.* (The words "singing" and "whistling" are simply reversed.) Either use an exact quote or paraphrase in ways that are clearly different from the author's wording.
Joe Blow was a happy man. (no citation)	**Wrong:** There are two problems here. First, it's an exact quote so it should be quoted *and* cited. Second, even if the quote were modified slightly, Scrivener should still be cited because it is *his personal judgment* (and not a simple fact) that Joe Blow is happy.
Joe Blow often walked down the road whistling and singing. (no citation)	**Wrong:** Same two problems as the previous example: (1) exact words should be both quoted and cited; and (2) Scrivener's personal judgment needs to be credited to him.

Joe Blow appeared to be "a happy man" and often walked down the road whistling and singing.[99]	**Wrong:** Despite the citation, some of Scrivener's exact words are outside the quotation marks. That creates the misleading impression that the words are original, rather than Scrivener's. This is a small violation, like going a few miles over the speed limit. But if such miscitations occur often or include significant portions of text, then they can become serious cases of plagiarism.
"Joe Blow was an anxious man, who often ran down the road."[99]	**Wrong:** The quote is not accurate. According to Scrivener, Joe Blow was not anxious; he was "happy." And he didn't run, he "walked." Although this misquotation is not plagiarism, it is an error. You should quote properly, and your work should be reliable. If such mistakes are repeated, if they are seriously misleading, or, worst of all, if they appear to be intentional, they may be considered academic fraud. (Plagiarism is fraud, too, but a different kind.)
Joe Blow "walked down the road" quietly.[99]	**Wrong:** The words inside the partial quotation are accurate, but the word following it distorts Scrivener's plain meaning. Again, this is not plagiarism, but it does violate the basic principle of presenting materials fairly and accurately. If such mistakes are repeated or if they show consistent bias (for example, to prove Joe Blow is a quiet person or hates music), they may be considered a type of academic fraud. At the very least, they are misleading.

The table refers to single sentences, but some citation issues involve paragraphs or whole sections of your paper. Let's say you are writing about urban poverty and that William Julius Wilson's analysis of the subject is central to one section. Whether or not you quote Wilson directly, you should include several citations of his work in that section, reflecting its importance for your paper. You could accomplish the same thing by including an explanatory citation early in the section. The footnote might say, "My analysis in this section draws heavily on William Julius Wilson's work, particularly *The Truly Disadvantaged: The Inner City, the Underclass, and Public Policy* (Chicago: University of Chicago Press, 1987), 87–122." Or you could include a similar comment in the text itself. Of course, you still need to include citations for any direct quotes.

PARAPHRASING

When you paraphrase an author's sentence, don't veer too close to her words. That's plagiarism, *even if it's unintentional and even if you cite the author.*

So, what's the best technique for rephrasing a quote? Set aside the other author's text and think about the point *you* want to get across. Write it down in your own words (with a citation) and then compare your sentence to the author's original. If they contain several identical words or merely substitute a couple of synonyms, rewrite yours. Try to put aside the other author's distinctive language and rhythm as you write. That's sometimes hard because the original sticks in your mind or seems just right. Still, you have to try. Your sentences and paragraphs should look and sound different from anyone you cite.

If you have trouble rephrasing an idea in your own words, jot down a brief note to yourself stating the point you want to make. Then back away, wait a little while, and try again. When you begin rewriting, look at your brief note but *don't look at the author's original sentence.* Once you have finished, check your new sentence against the author's original. You may have to try several times to get it right. Don't keep using the same words again and again. Approach the sentence from a fresh angle. If you still can't solve the problem, give up and use a direct quote (perhaps a whole sentence, perhaps only a few key words). It should either be a direct quote or your distinctive rephrasing. It cannot be lip-synching.

Why not use direct quotes in the first place? Sometimes that's the best solution — when the author's language is compelling, or when it says something important about the writer. When Franklin Roosevelt spoke about the attack on Pearl Harbor, he told America: "Yesterday, December 7, 1941 — a date which will live in infamy — the United States was suddenly and deliberately attacked . . . ."[2] No one would want to paraphrase that. It's perfect as it is, and it's historically significant. When you analyze novels and poems, you'll want to quote extensively to reveal the author's creative expression. Other phrases speak volumes about the people who utter them. That's why you might quote Islamic fundamentalists calling the United States "the Great Satan" or George W. Bush responding that they are "evil." These quotes convey the flavor of the conflict.

Because there are so many times when direct quotations are essential, you should avoid them where they're not. Overuse cheapens their value. Don't trot them out to express ordinary thoughts in ordinary words. Paraphrase. Just remember the basic rules: Cite the source and don't mimic the original language.

These rules apply to the whole academic community, from freshmen to faculty. A senior professor at the U.S. Naval Academy was recently stripped of tenure for violating them. Although Brian VanDeMark had written several well-regarded books, his *Pandora's Keepers: Nine Men and the Atomic Bomb* (2003) contains numerous passages that closely resemble other books.[3] Most were footnoted, but, as you now know, that doesn't eliminate the problem.[4]

Here are a few of the questionable passages, compiled by Robert Norris. (Norris compiled an even longer list of similarities between VanDeMark's work and his own 2002 book *Racing for the Bomb*.)[5]

---

2. President Franklin D. Roosevelt, Joint Address to Congress Leading to a Declaration of War Against Japan, December 8, 1941, http://www.fdrlibrary.marist.edu/oddec7 .html. Accessed June 1, 2004.

3. Brian VanDeMark, *Pandora's Keepers: Nine Men and the Atomic Bomb* (Boston: Little, Brown, 2003).

4. Jacques Steinberg, "U.S. Naval Academy Demotes Professor Over Copied Work," *New York Times* (national edition), October 29, 2003, A23.

5. Robert Norris, *Racing for the Bomb: General Leslie R. Groves, the Manhattan Project's Indispensable Man* (South Royalton, VT: Steerforth Press, 2002); Robert Norris, "Parallels with Richard Rhodes's Books [referring to Brian VanDeMark's *Pandora's Keepers*]," History News Network Web site, http://hnn.us/articles/1485.html. Accessed June 22, 2004. For convenience, I have rearranged the last two rows in the table, without changing the words.

BRIAN VANDEMARK, *PANDORA'S KEEPERS* (2003)	RICHARD RHODES, *THE MAKING OF THE ATOMIC BOMB* (1986) AND *DARK SUN* (1995)
". . . Vannevar Bush. A fit man of fifty-two who looked uncannily like a beardless Uncle Sam, Bush was a shrewd Yankee . . ." (60)	"Vannevar Bush made a similar choice that spring. The sharp-eyed Yankee engineer, who looked like a beardless Uncle Sam, had left his MIT vice presidency . . ." (*Making of the Atomic Bomb*, 336)
"Oppenheimer wondered aloud if the dead at Hiroshima and Nagasaki were not luckier than the survivors, whose exposure to radiation would have painful and lasting effects." (194–195)	"Lawrence found Oppenheimer weary, guilty and depressed, wondering if the dead at Hiroshima and Nagasaki were not luckier than the survivors, whose exposure to the bombs would have lifetime effects." (*Dark Sun*, 203)
"To toughen him up and round him out, Oppenheimer's parents had one of his teachers, Herbert Smith, take him out West during the summer before he entered Harvard College." (82)	"To round off Robert's convalescence and toughen him up, his father arranged for a favorite English teacher at Ethical Culture, a warm, supportive Harvard graduate named Herbert Smith, to take him out West for the summer." (*The Making of the Atomic Bomb*, 120–121)
"For the next three months, both sides marshaled their forces. At Strauss's request, the FBI tapping of Oppenheimer's home and office phones continued. The FBI also followed the physicist whenever he left Princeton." (259)	"For the next three months, both sides marshaled their forces. The FBI tapped Oppenheimer's home and office phones at Strauss's specific request and followed the physicist whenever he left Princeton." (*Dark Sun*, 539)

Source: Robert Norris, "Parallels with Richard Rhodes's Books [referring to Brian Van-DeMark's *Pandora's Keepers*], History News Network Web site, http://hnn.us/articles/1485.html. Accessed June 22, 2004. For convenience, I have rearranged the last two rows in the table, without changing the words.

Unfortunately, VanDeMark does not cite Rhodes or quote him directly in any of these passages. Some, like the last one, are virtual quotations and would raise red flags even if they occurred only once. A few others are a little too close for comfort, but raise problems mostly because there are so many of them in VanDeMark's book.[6] This is only one of several tables, covering VanDeMark's poor paraphrasing or unquoted sources. Each was prepared by a different author who felt violated. According to the Naval Academy's academic dean, "The whole approach to documenting the sources of the book was flawed."[7] The dean and VanDeMark himself attributed the problem to sloppiness rather than purposeful theft (which is why VanDeMark was demoted rather than fired outright). Still, the punishment was severe and shows how seriously plagiarism is taken at every level of the university.

PLAGIARIZING IDEAS

Plagiarizing doesn't just mean borrowing someone else's words. It also means borrowing someone else's ideas. Let's say you are impressed by an article comparing *Catcher in the Rye* and *Hamlet*.[8] The article concludes that these works are variations on a single theme: a young man's profound an-

----

6. Besides copying words and phrases from Richard Rhodes and Robert Norris, VanDeMark took passages from Greg Herken, William Lanouette, and Mary Palevsky without proper quotations or full attribution. Some passages are *not* obvious cases of plagiarism—deliberate or accidental—but some are nearly identical to other works and still others are too close for comfort. The overall pattern is troubling.

These parallels between VanDeMark's work and other books are documented online with similar tables. See History News Network, "Brian VanDeMark: Accused of Plagiarism," May 31, 2003, http://hnn.us/articles/1477.html. Accessed February 26, 2004. That page links to several tables comparing VanDeMark's wording to various authors'.

7. Nelson Hernández, "Scholar's Tenure Pulled for Plagiarism: Acts Not Deliberate, Naval Academy Says," *Washington Post*, October 29, 2003, B06, http://www.washington post.com/wp-dyn/articles/A32551–2003Oct28.html (accessed March 5, 2004).

8. Although I thought of this comparison between Hamlet and Holden Caulfield myself, I suspected others had, too. Just to be on the safe side, I decided to do a Google search. The top item offered to sell me a term paper on the subject! After this depressing discovery, I decided to search for "Catcher in the Rye + phony." I was deluged with offers. What a delicious irony: to buy a term paper on Holden Caulfield's hatred of all things phony.

guish and mental instability, as shown through his troubled internal mono-logues. If your paper incorporates this striking idea, credit the author who proposed it, *even if every word you say about it is your own.* Otherwise, your paper will wrongly imply you came up with the idea yourself. Holden Caulfield would call you a phony. The moral of the tale: It's perfectly fine to draw on others' ideas, as long as you give them credit. The only exception is when the ideas are commonplace.

DISTORTING IDEAS

A recurrent theme of this chapter is that you should acknowledge others' words and ideas and represent them faithfully, without distortion. When you paraphrase them, you should keep the author's meaning, even if you disagree with it. When you shorten a quote, you should indicate that you've shortened it and keep the essential idea.

There are really two goals here. The first is to maintain honesty in your own work. The second is to engage others' ideas fully, on a level playing field. That's the best way to confront diverse ideas, whether you agree with them or not. That's fair play, of course, but it's more than that. It's how you make your own work better. You are proving the mettle of your approach by passing a tough, fair test — one that compares your ideas to others without stacking the deck in your favor.

The danger to avoid is setting up flimsy straw men so you can knock them down without much effort. That's not only dishonest; it's intellectually lazy. Believe me, your own position will be much stronger and more effective if you confront the best opposing arguments, presented fairly, and show why yours is better.

CONCLUSION: THE RIGHT WAY TO PARAPHRASE AND CITE

The rules for paraphrasing and citation are based on a few core ideas:

- You are responsible for your written work, including the ideas, facts, and interpretations you include.
- Unless you say otherwise, every word you write is assumed to be your own.
- When you rely on others' work or ideas, acknowledge it openly.
  - When you use their ideas or data, give them credit.

- ○ When you use their exact words, use quotation marks plus a citation.
- ○ When you paraphrase, use your own distinctive voice and cite the original source. Make sure your language doesn't mimic the original. If it still does after rewriting, then use direct quotes.
- When you draw on others' work, present it fairly. No distortions. No straw men.
- When you present empirical material, show where you acquired it so others can check the data for themselves. (The exception is commonly known material, which does not need to be cited.)

These principles of fairness and disclosure are more than simple rules for citation. They are more than just "good housekeeping" in your paper. They are fundamental rules for academic integrity. They promote real learning. They apply to teachers and students alike and encourage free, fair, and open discussion of ideas — the heart and soul of a university.

Citations
A Quick Guide

• • • • • • • • • • • •

In the chapters to come, I'll cover citation styles in nearly every field. If the world were simple, they'd all be the same. In fact, each one has its little idiosyncrasies, its own twists and turns. Fortunately, none of them is complicated.

Chapter 4 covers the basics of citation for all fields. It deals with issues that crop up no matter which style you use.

After that, I'll describe each style in its own chapter. Each chapter shows you exactly how to cite the works you'll use, whether it's a journal article, the second volume of a three-volume work, an online newspaper, or a Web site. Because each style (or each format — they mean the same thing) is presented separately, you only need to turn to one chapter when you write a paper.

Which style should you use? That depends on which field your paper is in, what your professor suggests, and which one you prefer. If your paper is in the humanities, you'll use either Chicago or MLA citations. If it's in the social sciences, engineering, education, or business, you'll use either Chicago or APA. The biological sciences, chemistry, physics, mathematics, and computer sciences have their own individual styles and sometimes more than one per field. I'll cover each one and include plenty of examples.

I'll also cover legal citations, which have a style all their own.

In the final chapter, I'll answer some frequently asked questions dealing with all types of citations, in all styles. For example, should you cite your background readings? How many sources should your paper have? Can you include analysis in your footnotes?

Now, on to the basics of citation and, after that, the specifics of each style.

THE BASICS OF CITATION

4

. . . .

Acknowledging your sources is crucial to doing honest academic work. That means citing them properly, using one of several styles. The one you choose depends on your field, your professor's advice, and your own preferences.

There are three major citation styles:

- Chicago (or Turabian), used in many fields
- MLA, used in the humanities
- APA, used in social sciences, education, engineering, and business

Several sciences have also developed their own distinctive styles:

- CSE for the biological sciences
- AMA for the biomedical sciences, medicine, and nursing
- ACS for chemistry
- AIP for physics, plus other styles for astrophysics and astronomy
- AMS for mathematics and computer sciences

Legal citations are different from any of these.

I will cover each one, providing clear directions and plenty of examples so you won't have any trouble writing correct citations. That way, you can concentrate on your paper, not on the type of citation you're using. I'll cover each style separately so you can turn directly to the one you need. Using this information, you'll be able to cite books, articles, Web sites, films, musical performances, government documents — whatever you use in your papers.

Why would you ever want to use different citation styles? Why can't you just pick one and stick with it? Because different fields won't let you. They have designed citation styles to meet their special needs, whether it's genetics or German, and you'll just have to use them. In some sciences, for instance, proper citations list only the author, journal, and pages. They omit the article's title. If you did that in the humanities or social sciences, you'd be marked incorrect because proper citations for those fields *require* the title. Go figure.

Compare these bibliographic citations for an article of mine:

Chicago   Lipson, Charles. "Why Are Some International Agreements Informal?" *International Organization* 45 (Autumn 1991): 495–538.

APA   Lipson, C. (1991). Why are some international agreements informal? *International Organization, 45,* 495–538.

ACS   Lipson, C. *Int. Org.* **1991**, 45, 495.

None of these is complicated, but they *are* different. When you leave the chemistry lab to take a course on Shakespeare, you'll leave behind your citation style as well as your beakers. Not to worry. For chemistry papers, just turn to chapter 10. For Shakespeare, turn to chapter 6, which covers MLA citations for the humanities. Both chapters include lots of examples, presented in simple tables, so it won't be "double, double toil and trouble."

Despite their differences, *all these citation styles have the same basic goals*:

- to identify and credit the sources you use; and
- to give readers specific information so they can go to these sources themselves, if they wish.

Fortunately, the different styles include a lot of the same information. That means you can write down the same things as you take notes, without worrying about what kind of citations you will ultimately use. You should write down that information as soon as you start taking notes on a new book or article. If you photocopy an article, write all the reference information on the first page. If you do it first, you won't forget. You'll need it later for citations.

How these citations will ultimately look depends on which style you use. Chicago notes are either complete citations or shortened versions plus a complete description in the bibliography or in a previous note. Their name comes from their original source, *The Chicago Manual of Style,* published by the University of Chicago Press. This format is sometimes called

"Turabian" after a popular book based on that style, Kate Turabian's *A Manual for Writers of Term Papers, Theses, and Dissertations.*[1]

If you use complete-citation notes, you might not need a bibliography at all since the first note for each item includes all the necessary data. If you use the shortened form, though, you definitely need a bibliography since the notes skip vital information.

Whether you use complete-citation notes or the shortened version, you can place them either at the bottom of each page or the end of the document. Footnotes and endnotes are identical, except for their placement. Footnotes appear on the same page as the citation in the text. Endnotes are bunched together at the end of the paper, article, chapter, or book. Word processors give you an easy choice between the two.

MLA, APA, and the science citation styles were developed to provide alternative ways of referencing materials. They use in-text citations such as (Stewart 154) or (Stewart, 2004) with full information provided only in a reference list at the end.[2] Because these in-text citations are brief, they require a full bibliography. I'll describe each style in detail and provide lots of examples, just as I will for Chicago citations.

In case you are wondering about the initials: APA stands for the American Psychological Association, which uses this style in its professional journals. MLA stands for the Modern Language Association. Both styles have been adopted well beyond their original fields. APA is widely used in the social sciences, MLA in the humanities. Chicago citations are widely used in both. I will discuss the science styles (and what their initials mean) a little later.

Your department, school, or adviser may prefer one style, or even require it, or they might leave it up to you. Check on that as soon as you begin handing in papers with citations. Why not do it consistently from the beginning?

---

1. Kate Turabian, *A Manual for Writers of Term Papers, Theses, and Dissertations,* 6th ed. (Chicago: University of Chicago Press, 1996); *The Chicago Manual of Style,* 15th ed. (Chicago: University of Chicago Press, 2003).

2. Reference lists are similar to bibliographies, but there are some technical differences. In later chapters, I'll explain the details (and nomenclature) for each style. To avoid needless proliferation of citation styles, I include only the most common ones in each academic field. That means I leave out others, such as Turabian's shortened citations.

Tip on selecting a citation style: Check with your teachers in each class to find out what style citations they prefer. Then use that style consistently.

Speaking of consistency . . . it's an important aspect of footnoting. Stick with the same abbreviations, capitalizations, and don't mix styles within a paper. It's easy to write "Volume" in one footnote, "Vol." in another, and "vol." in a third. We all do it, and then we have to correct it. We all abbreviate "chapter" as both "chap." and "ch." Just try your best the first time around and then go back and fix the mistakes when you revise. That's why they invented the search-and-replace function.

My goal here is to provide a one-stop reference so that you can handle nearly all citation issues you'll face, regardless of which style you use and what kinds of items you cite. For each style, I'll show you how to cite books, articles, unpublished papers, Web sites, and lots more. For specialized documents, such as musical scores or scientific preprints, I show citations only in the fields that actually use them. Physicists often cite preprints, but they don't cite Beethoven. The physics chapter reflects those needs. Students in the humanities not only cite Beethoven; they cite dance performances, plays, and poems. I have included MLA citations for all of them. In case you need to cite something well off the beaten path, I'll explain where to find additional information for each style.

HANGING INDENTS

One final point about shared bibliographic style. Most bibliographies — Chicago, MLA, APA, and some of the sciences — use a special style known as "hanging indents." This applies only to the bibliography and not to footnotes or endnotes. It is the opposite of regular paragraph indention, where the first line is indented and the rest are regular length. In a hanging indent, the first line of each citation is regular length and the rest are indented. For example:

Rothenberg, Gunther E. "Maurice of Nassau, Gustavus Adolphus, Raimondo Montecuccoli, and the 'Military Revolution' of the Seventeenth Century." In *Makers of Modern Strategy from Machiavelli to the Nuclear Age,* edited by Peter Paret, 32–63. Princeton, NJ: Princeton University Press, 1986.

Spooner, Frank C. *Risks at Sea: Amsterdam Insurance and Maritime Europe, 1766–1780.* Cambridge: Cambridge University Press, 1983.

There's a good reason for this unusual format. Hanging indents are designed to make it easy to skim down the list of references and see the authors' names. To remind you to use this format, I'll use it myself when I illustrate references in the citation styles that use it. (The only ones that don't use hanging indents are science styles with numbered citations. It's actually not complicated, and I'll explain it later.)

To make the authors' names stand out further, most bibliographies list their last names first. If an author's name is repeated, however, the styles differ. APA repeats the full name for each citation. MLA uses three hyphens, followed by a period. Chicago uses three em dashes (that is, long dashes), followed by a period.[3]

Lipson, Charles. *Barbecue, Cole Slaw, and Extra Hot Sauce.* Midnight, MS: Hushpuppy, 2004.
———. *More Gumbo, Please.* Thibodeaux, LA: Andouille Press, 2003.

You can arrange hanging indents easily on your word processor. Go to the format feature and, within it, the section on paragraphs. Choose hanging indentation instead of regular or none.

WHERE TO FIND MORE

So far, we have covered some basic issues that apply to most citation styles. There are, of course, lots more questions, some that apply to all styles and some that apply only to one or two. Rather than cover these questions now, I'll handle them in the chapters on individual citation styles and in a final chapter on Frequently Asked Questions (FAQs).

If you have questions that aren't covered in the chapter on your citation style, be sure to check the FAQ chapter. If you still have questions, you can always go to the reference books for each style. Most styles have them (but not all). I'll list them in the chapters for individual styles.

---

3. Because em dashes are longer than hyphens, they show up differently on-screen and in print. The em dashes show up as a solid line, the hyphens as separate dashes. Three em dashes: ———. Three hyphens: ---. Frankly, you don't need to worry about this for your papers. Use the preferred one if you can, but either is fine.

ON TO THE NUTS AND BOLTS

I have organized the references so they are most convenient for you, putting all the documentation for each style in its own chapter.

Chapter 5: Chicago (or Turabian) citations
Chapter 6: MLA citations for the humanities
Chapter 7: APA citations for the social sciences, education, engineering, and business
Chapter 8: CSE citations for the biological sciences
Chapter 9: AMA citations for the biomedical sciences, medicine, and nursing
Chapter 10: ACS citations for chemistry
Chapter 11: Physics, astrophysics, and astronomy citations
Chapter 12: Mathematics and computer science citations
Chapter 13: *Bluebook* legal citations

Fortunately, they're very straightforward. They're mostly examples, showing you how to cite specific kinds of sources, such as the third edition of a popular book or a chapter in an edited volume. I've included lots of examples of electronic documents, too, from Weblogs and databases to electronic versions of print documents.

Don't bother trying to memorize any of these styles. There are simply too many minor details. Just follow the tables, and you'll be able to handle different sources — from journal articles to Web pages — in whichever style you need to use. Later, as you write more papers, you'll become familiar with the style you use most.

After explaining each style, I'll answer some common questions that apply to all of them. That's in chapter 14. Now, let's see how to do citations and bibliographies in the specific style you want to use.

5

CHICAGO (OR TURABIAN) CITATIONS

. . . .

Chicago citations are based on the authoritative *Chicago Manual of Style.* The manual, now in its fifteenth edition, is the bible for references and academic style. A briefer version, covering most aspects of student papers, is Kate Turabian's *A Manual for Writers of Term Papers, Theses, and Dissertations.*[1] This chapter, however, should cover all you need to document your sources, even if they're unusual.

THE CHICAGO MANUAL OF STYLE: FULL NOTES, SHORT NOTES, AND BIBLIOGRAPHY

Chicago-style notes come in two flavors, and I include both in this chapter.[2]

1. A complete first note + short follow-up notes.
   The first note for any item is a full one, giving complete information about the book, article, or other document. Subsequent entries for that item are brief. There is no need for a bibliography since all the information is covered in the first note.

---

1. Kate Turabian, *A Manual for Writers of Term Papers, Theses, and Dissertations,* 6th ed. (Chicago: University of Chicago Press, 1996); *The Chicago Manual of Style,* 15th ed. (Chicago: University of Chicago Press, 2003).

2. *The Chicago Manual of Style* and Turabian also describe another style, the author-date system. These citations appear in parentheses in the text, listing the author and the date of publication. For example: (Larmore 2004). Full citations appear in a reference list at the end. For simplicity, I have omitted this style since it is similar to APA, discussed in chapter 7.

- References are marked by superscript numbers in the text, such as this one.[99]
- Notes may appear at the bottom of the page or the end of the article, chapter, or book. These footnotes and endnotes are identical except for their location. In either location, the notes are identified with a superscript number.
- The first note includes all essential information for the work cited.
- Subsequent notes about that particular work are brief, containing only the author's last name, a short version of the title, and the pages cited. For example: Wood, *American Revolution*, 51–55.
- Both short notes and full notes may contain commentary. In fact, the note can be entirely commentary, if you wish. Or you can combine comments with references to books and articles in the same note.
- Since the first note contains an item's essential bibliographic data, there is no need for a separate bibliography at the end. If you wish to include one, though, you certainly can.

2. Short notes only + bibliography.

All notes are brief. Full information about the sources appears only in the bibliography.

- References are marked the same way as full notes, with superscript numbers like this[99] in the text.
- Shortened notes include only the author's last name, a brief title, and page number: Lipson, *Reliable Partners*, 12. *All* notes are shortened like this, including the first citation of an item.
- Shortened notes, like the full versions, may be either footnotes or endnotes. Like the full versions, they may contain commentary or even be entirely commentary.
- A bibliography, containing complete information about each item, is required. It uses hanging indents.

This means there are three ways to cite individual items. All of them are illustrated in this chapter.

A. Full first notes
B. Short notes
C. Bibliographic entries

The first flavor combines (A + B), the second combines (B + C).

This chapter covers everything from edited books to reference works, from sheet music to online databases, and lots of things in between. To make it easy to find what you need, I've listed them here alphabetically, together with the pages they are on. At the end of the chapter, I answer some question about using this style.

INDEX OF CHICAGO CITATIONS IN THIS CHAPTER

CHICAGO MANUAL OF STYLE: NOTES AND BIBLIOGRAPHY

Book, one author	Full first note	[99] Charles Lipson, *Reliable Partners: How Democracies Have Made a Separate Peace* (Princeton, NJ: Princeton University Press, 2003), 22–23. ‣ This is note number 99 and refers to pages 22–23. ‣ Footnotes and endnotes do not have hanging indents. Only the bibliography does.
	Short note	[99] Lipson, *Reliable Partners*, 22–23. ‣ Shorten titles to four words or less, if possible.
	Bibliography	Lipson, Charles. *Reliable Partners: How Democracies Have Made a Separate Peace.* Princeton, NJ: Princeton University Press, 2003.
Books, several by same author	First note	[99] Gerhard L. Weinberg, *Germany, Hitler, and World War II: Essays in Modern German and World History* (Cambridge: Cambridge University Press, 1995). [100] Gerhard L. Weinberg, *A World at Arms: A Global History of World War II* (Cambridge: Cambridge University Press, 1994).
	Short note	[99] Weinberg, *Germany, Hitler, and World War II.* [100] Weinberg, *World at Arms.*
	Bibliography	Weinberg, Gerhard L. *Germany, Hitler, and World War II: Essays in Modern German and World History.* Cambridge: Cambridge University Press, 1995. ———. *A World at Arms: A Global History of World War II.* Cambridge: Cambridge University Press, 1994. ‣ The repetition of the author's name uses three em dashes (which are simply long dashes), followed by a period. You can find em dashes by digging around in Microsoft Word. Go to "Insert," then "Symbols," then "Special Characters." After you do it once, you can simply copy and paste it. If, for some reason, you can't find the em dashes, just use three hyphens. ‣ List works for each author alphabetically, by title.

Book, multiple authors	First note	⁹⁹ Dan Reiter and Allan C. Stam, *Democracies at War* (Princeton, NJ: Princeton University Press, 2002), 15–26.
	Short note	⁹⁹ Reiter and Stam, *Democracies at War*, 15–26. ▸ Titles with four words or less are not shortened.
	Bibliography	Reiter, Dan, and Allan C. Stam. *Democracies at War*. Princeton, NJ: Princeton University Press, 2002. ▸ List up to ten coauthors in the bibliography. If there are more, list the first seven, followed by "et al."

Book, multiple editions	First note	⁹⁹ William Strunk Jr. and E. B. White, *The Elements of Style*, 4th ed. (New York: Longman, 2000), 12.
	Short note	⁹⁹ Strunk and White, *Elements of Style*, 12. ▸ To keep the note short, the title doesn't include the initial article (~~The~~ *Elements of Style*) or the edition number.
	Bibliography	Strunk, William, Jr., and E. B. White. *The Elements of Style*. 4th ed. New York: Longman, 2000.

Book, edited	First note	⁹⁹ Francis Robinson, ed., *Cambridge Illustrated History of the Islamic World* (Cambridge: Cambridge University Press, 1996). ⁹⁹ David Taras, Frits Pannekoek, and Maria Bakardjieva, eds., *How Canadians Communicate* (Calgary, AB: University of Calgary Press, 2003). ▸ Use standard two-letter abbreviations for Canadian provinces.
	Short note	⁹⁹ Robinson, *History of Islamic World*. ▸ Choose the most relevant words when shortening the title. Also, drop the abbreviation for editor. ⁹⁹ Taras, Pannekoek, and Bakardjieva, *How Canadians Communicate*.

Book, edited *(continued)*	Bibliography	Robinson, Francis, ed. *Cambridge Illustrated History of the Islamic World*. Cambridge: Cambridge University Press, 1996. Taras, David, Frits Pannekoek, and Maria Bakardjieva, eds. *How Canadians Communicate*. Calgary, AB: University of Calgary Press, 2003.
Book, anonymous or no author	First note	[99] Anonymous, *Through Our Enemies' Eyes: Osama Bin Laden, Radical Islam, and the Future of America* (Washington, DC: Brassey's, 2003). [99] *Golden Verses of the Pythagoreans* (Whitefish, MT: Kessinger, 2003).
	Short note	[99] Anonymous, *Through Our Enemies' Eyes*. [99] *Golden Verses of Pythagoreans*.
	Bibliography	Anonymous, *Through Our Enemies' Eyes: Osama Bin Laden, Radical Islam, and the Future of America*. Washington, DC: Brassey's, 2003. *Golden Verses of the Pythagoreans*. Whitefish, MT: Kessinger, 2003. ▸ If a book lists "anonymous" as the author, then that name should be included. If no author is listed, then you may list "anonymous" or simply begin with the title.
Book, online	First note	[99] Charles Dickens, *Great Expectations* (1860–61; Project Gutenberg, 1998), etext 1400, http://www.gutenberg.net/etext98/grexp10.txt. ▸ The etext number is helpful but not essential.
	Short note	[99] Dickens, *Great Expectations*.
	Bibliography	Dickens, Charles. *Great Expectations* (1860–61; Project Gutenberg, 1998). Etext 1400. http://www.gutenberg.net/etext98/grexp10.txt.
Multivolume work	First note	[99] Otto Pflanze, *Bismarck and the Development of Germany,* 3 vols. (Princeton, NJ: Princeton University Press, 1963–90), 1:153.
	Short note	[99] Pflanze, *Bismarck*, 1:153.

	Bibliography	Pflanze, Otto. *Bismarck and the Development of Germany.* 3 vols. Princeton, NJ: Princeton University Press, 1963–90.

Single volume in multivolume work	First note	[99] Otto Pflanze, *Bismarck and the Development of Germany*, vol. 3, *The Period of Fortification, 1880–1898* (Princeton, NJ: Princeton University Press, 1990), 237. [99] Akira Iriye, *The Globalizing of America*, Cambridge History of American Foreign Relations, edited by Warren I. Cohen, vol. 3 (Cambridge: Cambridge University Press, 1993), 124. ▸ Pflanze wrote all three volumes. Iriye wrote only the third volume in a series edited by Cohen.
	Short note	[99] Pflanze, *Bismarck*, 3:237. [99] Iriye, *Globalizing of America*, 124.
	Bibliography	Pflanze, Otto. *Bismarck and the Development of Germany.* Vol. 3, *The Period of Fortification, 1880–1898*. Princeton, NJ: Princeton University Press, 1990. Iriye, Akira. *The Globalizing of America.* Cambridge History of American Foreign Relations, edited by Warren I. Cohen, vol. 3. Cambridge: Cambridge University Press, 1993.

Reprint of earlier edition	First note	[99] Jacques Barzun, *Simple and Direct: A Rhetoric for Writers*, rev. ed. (1985; repr., Chicago: University of Chicago Press, 1994), 27. [99] Adam Smith, *An Inquiry into the Nature and Causes of the Wealth of Nations* (1776), ed. Edwin Cannan (Chicago: University of Chicago Press, 1976).
	Short note	[99] Barzun, *Simple and Direct*, 27. [99] Smith, *Wealth of Nations*, vol. I, bk. IV, chap. II: 477. ▸ This modern edition of Smith is actually a single volume, but it retains the volume numbering of the 1776 original. You could simply cite the page

Reprint of earlier edition (*continued*)		number, but the full citation helps readers with other editions.
	Bibliography	Barzun, Jacques. *Simple and Direct: A Rhetoric for Writers*. 1985. Chicago: University of Chicago Press, 1994. Smith, Adam. *An Inquiry into the Nature and Causes of the Wealth of Nations*. 1776. Ed. Edwin Cannan. Chicago: University of Chicago Press, 1976.
Translated volume	First note	[99] Max Weber, *The Protestant Ethic and the Spirit of Capitalism* (1904–5), trans. Talcott Parsons (New York: Charles Scribner's Sons, 1958), 176–77. [99] Alexis de Tocqueville, *Democracy in America* (1835), ed. J. P. Mayer, trans. George Lawrence (New York: HarperCollins, 2000). ▸ Translator and editor are listed in the order they appear on the book's title page. [99] Seamus Heaney, trans., *Beowulf: A New Verse Translation* (New York: Farrar, Straus and Giroux, 2000). ▸ For *Beowulf,* the translator's name appears before the book title because Heaney's is the only name on the title page. (The poem is anonymous.) The same treatment would be given to an editor or compiler whose name appeared alone on the title page.
	Short note	[99] Weber, *Protestant Ethic*, 176–77. [99] Tocqueville, *Democracy in America*. [99] *Beowulf.* Or [99] Heaney, trans., *Beowulf.*
	Bibliography	Weber, Max. *The Protestant Ethic and the Spirit of Capitalism*. 1904–5. Trans. Talcott Parsons. New York: Charles Scribner's Sons, 1958. Tocqueville, Alexis de. *Democracy in America*. 1835. Ed. J. P. Mayer. Trans. George Lawrence. New York: HarperCollins, 2000. Heaney, Seamus, trans. *Beowulf: A New Verse Translation*. New York: Farrar, Straus and Giroux, 2000.

Chapter in edited book	First note	[99] Robert Keohane, "The Demand for International Regimes," in *International Regimes*, ed. Stephen Krasner, 55–67 (Ithaca, NY: Cornell University Press, 1983).
	Short note	[99] Keohane, "Demand for International Regimes," 56–67.
	Bibliography	Keohane, Robert. "The Demand for International Regimes." In *International Regimes*, edited by Stephen Krasner, 56–67. Ithaca, NY: Cornell University Press, 1983.
Journal article	First note	[99] Charles Lipson, "Why Are Some International Agreements Informal?" *International Organization* 45 (Autumn 1991): 495–538.
	Short note	[99] Lipson, "International Agreements," 495–538.
	Bibliography	Lipson, Charles. "Why Are Some International Agreements Informal?" *International Organization* 45 (Autumn 1991): 495–538.
Journal article, multiple authors	First note	[99] William G. Thomas III and Edward L. Ayers, "An Overview: The Differences Slavery Made: A Close Analysis of Two American Communities," *American Historical Review* 108 (December 2003): 1299–307.
	Short note	[99] Thomas and Ayers, "Differences Slavery Made," 1299–307.
	Bibliography	Thomas, William G., III, and Edward L. Ayers. "An Overview: The Differences Slavery Made: A Close Analysis of Two American Communities." *American Historical Review* 108 (December 2003): 1299–307.
Journal article online	First note	[99] Christopher Small, "Why Doesn't the Whole World Love Chamber Music?" *American Music* 19:3 (Autumn 2001): 340–59. http://links.jstor.org/sici?sici=0734-4392%28200123%2919%3A3%3C340%3AWDTWWL%3E2.0.CO%3B2-J (accessed March 15, 2004).

Journal article online (*continued*)	Short note	[99] Small, "Chamber Music," 340–59.
	Bibliography	Small, Christopher. "Why Doesn't the Whole World Love Chamber Music?" *American Music* 19:3 (Autumn 2001): 340–59. http://links .jstor.org/sici?sici=0734-4392%28200123 %2919%3A3%3C340%3AWDTWWL%3E2.0.CO %3B2-J (accessed March 15, 2004).
Newspaper or magazine article, no author	First note	[99] "Report of 9/11 Panel Cites Lapses by C.I.A. and F.B.I.," *New York Times*, July 23, 2003 (national edition), 1. ▸ This refers to page 1. ▸ If the article has a byline and you wish to include the reporter's name, you certainly can: David Johnston, "Report of 9/11 Panel. . . ." ▸ Short articles in newsweeklies like *Time* are treated the same as newspaper articles. Longer articles with bylines are treated like journal articles.
	Short note	[99] "Report of 9/11 Panel," *New York Times*, 1. ▸ Since newspapers are usually omitted from the bibliography, use a full citation for the first reference.
	Bibliography	▸ Newspapers articles are left out of bibliographies, but you can include an especially important article: "Report of 9/11 Panel Cites Lapses by C.I.A. and F.B.I." *New York Times*, July 23, 2003, national edition, 1.
Newspaper or magazine article, with author	First note	[99] Jason Horowitz, "Vatican Official Is Killed by Gunmen in Burundi," *New York Times*, December 30, 2003 (national edition), A9.
	Short note	[99] Horowitz, "Vatican Official Is Killed," A9.
	Bibliography	▸ Newspaper and magazine articles are rarely included in bibliographies.

Newspaper or magazine article online	First note	[99] Karl Vick, "Iranians Flee Quake-Devastated City," *Washington Post*, December 31, 2003, A01, http://www.washingtonpost.com/wp-dyn/articles/A42890-2003Dec30.html (accessed March 14, 2004).
	Short note	[99] Vick, "Iranians Flee Quake-Devastated City."
	Bibliography	► Rarely included.

Review	First note	[99] H. Allen Orr, "What's Not in Your Genes," review of *Nature via Nurture: Genes, Experience, and What Makes Us Human*, by Matt Ridley, *New York Review of Books* 50 (August 14, 2003): 38–40. [99] Zdravko Planinc, review of *Eros and Polis: Desire and Community in Greek Political Theory*, by Paul W. Ludwig, *Perspectives on Politics* 1 (December 2003): 764–65.
	Short note	[99] Orr, "What's Not in Your Genes." [99] Planinc, review of *Eros and Polis*.
	Bibliography	Orr, H. Allen. "What's Not in Your Genes." Review of *Nature via Nurture: Genes, Experience, and What Makes Us Human*, by Matt Ridley. *New York Review of Books* 50 (August 14, 2003): 38–40. Planinc, Zdravko. Review of *Eros and Polis: Desire and Community in Greek Political Theory*, by Paul W. Ludwig. *Perspectives on Politics* 1 (December 2003): 764–65.

Unpublished paper, thesis, or dissertation	First note	[99] Janice Bially-Mattern, "Ordering International Politics: Identity, Crisis, and Representational Force" (paper presented at the Program on International Politics, Economics, and Security, University of Chicago, February 5, 2004), 1–25. [99] Nicole Childs, "The Impact of Hurricane Floyd on the Children of Eastern North Carolina" (master's thesis, Eastern Carolina University, 2002), 24.

Unpublished paper, thesis, or dissertation (*continued*)		[99] Soon-Yong Choi, "Optimal Quality Choices: Product Selection in Cable Television Services" (PhD diss., University of Texas, Austin, 1996).
	Short note	[99] Bially-Mattern, "Ordering International Politics." [99] Childs, "Impact of Hurricane Floyd." [99] Choi, "Optimal Quality Choices."
	Bibliography	Bially-Mattern, Janice. "Ordering International Politics: Identity, Crisis, and Representational Force." Paper presented at the Program on International Politics, Economics, and Security, University of Chicago, February 5, 2004. Childs, Nicole. "The Impact of Hurricane Floyd on the Children of Eastern North Carolina." Master's thesis, Eastern Carolina University, 2002. Choi, Soon-Yong. "Optimal Quality Choices: Product Selection in Cable Television Services." PhD diss., University of Texas, Austin, 1996.
Preprint	First note	[99] Richard Taylor, "On the Meromorphic Continuation of Degree Two L-Functions," preprint, http://abel.math.harvard.edu/~rtaylor/ (accessed January 5, 2004).
	Short note	[99] Taylor, "Meromorphic Continuation."
	Bibliography	Taylor, Richard. "On the Meromorphic Continuation of Degree Two L-functions," preprint. http://abel.math.harvard.edu/~rtaylor/ (accessed January 5, 2004).
Microfilm, microfiche	First note	[99] Martin Luther King Jr., *FBI File*, ed. David J. Garrow (Frederick, MD: University Publications of America, 1984), microform, 16 reels. [99] Alice Irving Abbott, *Circumstantial Evidence* (New York: W. B. Smith, 1882), in *American Fiction, 1774–1910* (Woodbridge, CT: Gale/Primary Source Microfilm, 1998), reel A-1.

Short note	⁹⁹ King, *FBI File*, 11:23–24. ⁹⁹ Abbott, *Circumstantial Evidence*, 73.
Bibliography	King, Martin Luther Jr., *FBI File*. Ed. David J. Garrow. Frederick, MD: University Publications of America, 1984. Microform. 16 reels. Abbott, Alice Irving. *Circumstantial Evidence*. New York: W. B. Smith, 1882. In *American Fiction, 1774–1910*. Reel A-1. Woodbridge, CT: Gale/Primary Source Microfilm, 1998.

▶ You can omit any mention of microfilm or microfiche if it simply preserves a source in its original form. Just cite the work as if it were the published version. So, to cite the Abbott book:

Abbott, Alice Irving. *Circumstantial Evidence*. New York: W. B. Smith, 1882.

Encyclopedia, hard copy and online	First note

⁹⁹ *Encyclopaedia Britannica*, 15th ed., s.vv. "Balkans: History," "World War I."

▶ s.v. (*sub verbo*) means "under the word." Plural: s.vv.

▶ You must include the edition but, according to the *Chicago Manual of Style*, you can omit the publisher, location, and page numbers for well-known references like *Encyclopaedia Britannica*.

⁹⁹ *Encyclopaedia Britannica Online*, s.v. "Balkans," http://search.eb.com/eb/article?eu=119645 (accessed January 2, 2004).

⁹⁹ George Graham, "Behaviorism," in *Stanford Encyclopedia of Philosophy*, http://plato.stanford.edu/entries/behaviorism/ (accessed January 3, 2004).

▶ Or

⁹⁹ *Stanford Encyclopedia of Philosophy*, "Behaviorism" (by George Graham), in http://plato.stanford.edu/entries/behaviorism/ (accessed January 3, 2004).

Short note	⁹⁹ *Encyclopaedia Britannica*, s.v. "World War I." ⁹⁹ Graham, "Behaviorism." ⁹⁹ *Stanford Encyclopedia*, "Behaviorism."

Encyclopedia, hard copy and online (*continued*)	Bibliography	*Encyclopaedia Britannica.* 15th ed. s.vv. "Balkans: History." "World War I." *Encyclopaedia Britannica Online.* s.v. "Balkans," http://search.eb.com/eb/article?eu=119645 (accessed January 2, 2004). Graham, George. "Behaviorism," in *Stanford Encyclopedia of Philosophy.* http://plato.stanford.edu/entries/behaviorism/ (accessed January 3, 2004). ▸ Or *Stanford Encyclopedia of Philosophy.* "Behaviorism" (by George Graham). http://plato.stanford.edu/entries/behaviorism/ (accessed January 3, 2004).
Reference book, hard copy and online	First note	[99] *Reference Guide to World Literature*, 3rd ed., 2 vols., ed. Sara Pendergast and Tom Pendergast (Detroit: St. James Press/Thomson-Gale, 2003). [99] *Reference Guide to World Literature*, 3rd ed., ed. Sara Pendergast and Tom Pendergast, e-book (Detroit: St. James Press, 2003). [99] Edmund Cusick, "The Snow Queen, story by Hans Christian Andersen," in *Reference Guide to World Literature*, 3rd ed., 2 vols., ed. Sara Pendergast and Tom Pendergast (Detroit: St. James Press/Thomson-Gale, 2003), II:1511–12. [99] "Great Britain: Queen's Speech Opens Parliament," November 26, 2003, *FirstSearch*, Facts On File database, accession no. 2003302680.
	Short note	[99] *Reference Guide to World Literature*. [99] Cusick, "Snow Queen," II:1511–12. [99] "Great Britain: Queen's Speech."
	Bibliography	*Reference Guide to World Literature*. 3rd ed. 2 vols. Ed. Sara Pendergast and Tom Pendergast. Detroit: St. James Press/Thomson-Gale, 2003. *Reference Guide to World Literature*. 3rd ed. Ed. Sara Pendergast and Tom Pendergast. E-book. Detroit: St. James Press, 2003. Cusick, Edmund. "The Snow Queen, story by

Hans Christian Andersen." In *Reference Guide to World Literature*. 3rd ed. 2 vols. Ed. Sara Pendergast and Tom Pendergast, II:1511–12. Detroit: St. James Press/Thomson-Gale, 2003.

"Great Britain: Queen's Speech Opens Parliament." November 26, 2003. *FirstSearch*. Facts On File database. Accession no. 2003302680.

Dictionary, hard copy, online, or CD-ROM	First note	[99] *Merriam-Webster's Collegiate Dictionary*, 11th ed., s.v. "chronology."

▸ You must include the edition but can omit the publisher, location, and page numbers for well-known references like *Merriam-Webster's*.

[99] *Compact Edition of the Oxford English Dictionary*, s.vv. "class, *n.*," "state, *n.*"

▸ The words "class" and "state" can be either nouns or verbs, and this reference is to the nouns.

[99] Dictionary.com, s.v. "status," http://dictionary.reference.com/search?q=status (accessed February 2, 2004).

[99] *American Heritage Dictionary of the English Language*, 4th ed., CD-ROM.

Short note

[99] *Merriam-Webster's*, s.v. "chronology."
[99] *Compact O.E.D.*, s.vv. "class, *n.*," "state, *n.*"
[99] Dictionary.com, s.v. "status."
[99] *American Heritage Dictionary of the English Language* on CD-ROM.

Bibliography

▸ Standard dictionaries are not normally listed in bibliographies, but you may wish to include more specialized reference works:

Middle English Dictionary, W.2, ed. Robert E. Lewis. Ann Arbor: University of Michigan Press, 1999.

Medieval English Dictionary online. s.v. "boidekin." http://ets.umdl.umich.edu/cgi/m/mec/med-idx?type=id&id=MED5390.

Bible	**First note**	[99] Genesis 1:1, 1:3–5, 2:4.
		[99] Genesis 1:1, 1:3–5, 2:4 (New Revised Standard Version).
		► Books of the Bible can be abbreviated: Gen. 1:1.
		► Abbreviations for the next four books are Exod., Lev., Num., and Deut. Abbreviations for other books are easily found with a Web search for "abbreviations + Bible."
	Short note	[99] Genesis 1:1, 1:3–5, 2:4.
	Bibliography	► Biblical references are not normally included in the bibliography, but you may wish to include a particular version or translation:
		Tanakh: The Holy Scriptures: The New JPS Translation According to the Traditional Hebrew Text. Philadelphia: Jewish Publication Society, 1985.
		► Thou shalt omit the Divine Author's name.
Speech, academic talk, or course lecture	**First note**	[99] Henry S. Bienen, "State of the University Speech" (Northwestern University, Evanston, IL, March 6, 2003).
		[99] Theda Skocpol, "Voice and Inequality: The Transformation of American Civic Democracy" (Presidential address, American Political Science Association convention, Philadelphia, PA, August 28, 2003).
		[99] Gary Sick, lecture on U.S. policy toward Iraq (course on U.S. Foreign Policy Making in the Persian Gulf, Columbia University, New York, March 14, 2004).
		► The title of Professor Sick's talk is not in quotes because it is a regular course lecture and does not have a specific title. I have given a description, but you could simply call it a lecture and omit the description. For example: Gary Sick, lecture (course on U.S. Foreign . . .).
	Short note	[99] Bienen, "State of the University Speech."
		► Or, to differentiate it from Bienen's 2002 talk:
		[99] Bienen, "State of the University Speech," 2003.
		[99] Skocpol, "Voice and Inequality."
		[99] Sick, lecture on U.S. policy toward Iraq.

	Bibliography	Bienen, Henry S. "State of the University Speech." Northwestern University, Evanston, IL, March 6, 2003.
		Skocpol, Theda. "Voice and Inequality: The Transformation of American Civic Democracy," Presidential address, American Political Science Association convention, Philadelphia, PA, August 28, 2003.
		Sick, Gary. Lecture on U.S. policy toward Iraq. Course on U.S. Foreign Policy Making in the Persian Gulf, Columbia University, New York, March 14, 2004.
Interview: personal, telephone, or in print	First note	[99] V. S. Naipaul, personal interview, January 14, 2004.
		[99] Tony Blair, telephone interview, February 16, 2004.
		[99] Gloria Macapagal Arroyo, "A Time for Prayer," interview by Michael Schuman, *Time*, July 28, 2003, http://www.time.com/time/nation/article/0,8599,471205,00.html.
	Short note	[99] Naipaul, personal interview.
		[99] Blair, telephone interview.
		[99] Arroyo, "Time for Prayer."
	Bibliography	Naipaul, V. S. Personal interview. January 14, 2004.
		Blair, Tony. Telephone interview. February 16, 2004.
		Arroyo, Gloria Macapagal. "A Time for Prayer." Interview by Michael Schuman. *Time*. July 28, 2003. http://www.time.com/time/nation/article/0,8599,471205,00.html.
Poem	First note	[99] Elizabeth Bishop, "The Fish," *The Complete Poems, 1927–1979* (New York: Noonday Press/Farrar, Straus and Giroux, 1983), 42–44.
	Short note	[99] Bishop, "The Fish," 42–44.
	Bibliography	Bishop, Elizabeth. "The Fish." *The Complete Poems, 1927–1979*, 42–44. New York: Noonday Press/Farrar, Straus and Giroux, 1983.

Play	First note	[99] Shakespeare, *Romeo and Juliet*, 2.1.1–9.
		▸ Refers to act 2, scene 1, lines 1–9. If you wish to cite a specific edition, then:
		[99] Shakespeare, *Romeo and Juliet*, ed. Brian Gibbons (London: Methuen, 1980).
	Short note	[99] Shakespeare, *Romeo and Juliet*, 2.1.1–9.
	Bibliography	Shakespeare, *Romeo and Juliet*. Ed. Brian Gibbons. London: Methuen, 1980.

Performance of play or dance	First note	[99] *Kiss*, choreography Susan Marshall, music Arvo Pärt, perf. Cheryl Mann, Tobin Del Cuore, Hubbard Street Dance Chicago, Chicago, March 12, 2004.
		[99] *Topdog/Underdog*, by Suzan Lori-Parks, dir. Amy Morton, perf. K. Todd Freeman, David Rainey, Steppenwolf Theater, Chicago, November 2, 2003.
		▸ If you are concentrating on one person or one position such as director, put that person's name first. For example, if you are concentrating on David Rainey's acting:
		[99] David Rainey, perf., *Topdog/Underdog*, by Suzan Lori-Parks, dir. Amy Morton. . . .
	Short note	[99] *Kiss*.
		[99] *Topdog/Underdog*.
	Bibliography	*Kiss*. Choreography Susan Marshall. Music Arvo Pärt. Perf. Cheryl Mann, Tobin Del Cuore. Hubbard Street Dance Chicago, Chicago. March 12, 2004.
		Topdog/Underdog. By Suzan Lori-Parks. Dir. Amy Morton. Perf. K. Todd Freeman, David Rainey. Steppenwolf Theater, Chicago. November 2, 2003.
		▸ Or, if you are concentrating on Rainey's acting:
		Rainey, David, perf. *Topdog/Underdog*. By Suzan Lori-Parks. Dir. Amy Morton. . . .

Television program	First note	[99] *Seinfeld*, "The Soup Nazi," episode 116, November 2, 1995.
		▸ Or, a fuller citation:

[99] *Seinfeld*, "The Soup Nazi," episode 116, dir. Andy Ackerman, writer Spike Feresten, perf. Jerry Seinfeld, Jason Alexander, Julia Louis-Dreyfus, Michael Richards, Alexandra Wentworth, Larry Thomas, NBC, November 2, 1995.

Short note	[99] *Seinfeld*, "Soup Nazi."
Bibliography	*Seinfeld*, "The Soup Nazi." Episode 116. Dir. Andy Ackerman. Writer Spike Feresten. Perf. Jerry Seinfeld, Jason Alexander, Julia Louis-Dreyfus, Michael Richards, Alexandra Wentworth, Larry Thomas. NBC, November 2, 1995.

Film	First note	[99] *Godfather II*. DVD, dir. Francis Ford Coppola (1974; Los Angeles: Paramount Home Video, 2003).

- ▸ If you wish to cite individual scenes, which are accessible on DVDs, treat them like chapters in books. "Murder of Fredo," *Godfather II*. . . .

Short note	[99] *Godfather II*.
Bibliography	*Godfather II*. DVD. Dir. Francis Ford Coppola. Perf. Al Pacino, Robert De Niro, Robert Duvall, Diane Keaton. Screenplay by Francis Ford Coppola and Mario Puzo based on novel by Mario Puzo. 1974; Paramount Home Video, 2003.

- ▸ Title, director, studio, and year of release are all required. So is the year the video recording was released, if that's what you are citing.
- ▸ Optional: the actors, producers, screenwriters, editors, cinematographers, and other information. You can include what you need for your paper, in order of their importance to your analysis. Their names appear between the title and the distributor.

Artwork original	First note	[99] Jacopo Robusti Tintoretto, *The Birth of John the Baptist*, 1550s, Hermitage, St. Petersburg.

- ▸ The year of the painting is optional.

Artwork original *(continued)*	Short note	[99] Tintoretto, *Birth of John the Baptist.*
	Bibliography	Tintoretto, Jacopo Robusti. *The Birth of John the Baptist.* 1550s. Hermitage, St. Petersburg.
Artwork reproduction	First note	[99] Jacopo Robusti Tintoretto, *The Birth of John the Baptist*, 1550s, in Tom Nichols, *Tintoretto: Tradition and Identity* (London: Reaktion Books, 1999), 47.
	Short note	[99] Tintoretto, *The Birth of John the Baptist.*
	Bibliography	Tintoretto, Jacopo Robusti. *The Birth of John the Baptist.* 1550s. In Tom Nichols, *Tintoretto: Tradition and Identity,* 47. London: Reaktion Books, 1999.
Artwork online	First note	[99] Jacopo Robusti Tintoretto, *The Birth of John the Baptist*, 1550s, Hermitage, St. Petersburg, http://www.hermitage.ru/html_En/index.html (accessed February 1, 2004). [99] Jacopo Robusti Tintoretto, *The Birth of John the Baptist* (detail), 1550s, Hermitage, St. Petersburg. http://cgfa.floridaimaging.com/t/p-tintore1.htm (accessed January 6, 2004).
	Short note	[99] Tintoretto, *The Birth of John the Baptist.*
	Bibliography	Tintoretto, Jacopo Robusti. *The Birth of John the Baptist.* 1550s. Hermitage, St. Petersburg. http://www.hermitage.ru/html_En/index.html (accessed February 1, 2004). Tintoretto, Jacopo Robusti. *The Birth of John the Baptist* (detail). 1550s. Hermitage, St. Petersburg. http://cgfa.floridaimaging.com/t/p-tintore1.htm (accessed January 6, 2004).
Photograph	First note	[99] Ansel Adams, *Monolith, the Face of Half Dome, Yosemite National Park*, 1927, Art Institute, Chicago.
	Short note	[99] Adams, *Monolith.*
	Bibliography	Adams, Ansel. *Monolith, the Face of Half Dome, Yosemite National Park.* 1927. Art Institute, Chicago.

Musical recording	First note	[99] Robert Johnson. "Cross Road Blues," 1937, *Robert Johnson: King of the Delta Blues Singers* (Columbia Records 1654, 1961). [99] Samuel Barber, "Cello Sonata, for cello and piano, Op. 6," in *Barber: Adagio for Strings, Violin Concerto, Orchestral and Chamber Works*, disc 2, St. Louis Symphony, Leonard Slatkin, cond.; Alan Stepansky, cello; Israela Margalit, piano (EMI Classics 74287, 2001).
	Short note	[99] Johnson. "Cross Road Blues." [99] Barber, "Cello Sonata, Op. 6."
	Bibliography	Johnson, Robert. "Cross Road Blues." *Robert Johnson: King of the Delta Blues Singers*. Columbia Records 1654, 1961. Barber, Samuel. "Cello Sonata, for cello and piano, Op. 6." *Barber: Adagio for Strings, Violin Concerto, Orchestral and Chamber Works*. Disc 2, St. Louis Symphony. Leonard Slatkin, cond.; Alan Stepansky, cello; Israela Margalit, piano. EMI Classics 74287, 2001.
Sheet music	First note	[99] Johann Sebastian Bach, "Toccata and Fugue in D Minor," 1708, BWV 565, arr. Ferruccio Benvenuto Busoni for solo piano (New York: G. Schirmer, LB1629, 1942).
	Short note	[99] Bach, "Toccata and Fugue in D Minor."
	Bibliography	Bach, Johann Sebastian. "Toccata and Fugue in D Minor." 1708. BWV 565. Arr. Ferruccio Benvenuto Busoni for solo piano. New York: G. Schirmer LB1629, 1942. ▸ This piece was written in 1708 and has the standard Bach classification BWV 565. This particular arrangement was published by G. Schirmer in 1942 and has their catalog number LB1629.
Liner notes	First note	[99] Steven Reich, liner notes for *Different Trains* (Elektra/Nonesuch 9 79176-2, 1988).

| Liner notes (*continued*) | Short note | [99] Reich, liner notes. Or
[99] Reich, liner notes, *Different Trains*. |
| | Bibliography | Reich, Steven. Liner notes for *Different Trains*. Elektra/Nonesuch 9 79176-2, 1988. |

Government document, hard copy and online	First note	[99] Senate Committee on Armed Services, *Hearings on S. 758, A Bill to Promote the National Security by Providing for a National Defense Establishment*, 80th Cong., 1st sess., 1947, S. Rep. 239, 13. ▸ "S. Rep. 239, 13" refers to report number 239, page 13. [99] Environmental Protection Agency (EPA), *Final Rule, Air Pollution Control: Prevention of Significant Deterioration; Approval and Promulgation of Implementation Plans*, Federal Register 68, no. 247 (December 24, 2003): 74483–91. [99] United States, Department of State. "China — 25th Anniversary of Diplomatic Relations," press statement, December 31, 2003, http://www.state.gov/r/pa/prs/ps/2003/27632.htm (accessed March 15, 2004).
	Short note	[99] Senate, *Hearings on S. 758*, 13. [99] EPA, *Final Rule, Air Pollution Control*. [99] State Department, "China — 25th Anniversary."
	Bibliography	U.S. Congress. Senate. Committee on Armed Services. *Hearings on S. 758, Bill to Promote the National Security by Providing for a National Defense Establishment*. 80th Cong., 1st sess., 1947. S. Rep. 239. Environmental Protection Agency. *Final Rule, Air Pollution Control: Prevention of Significant Deterioration; Approval and Promulgation of Implementation Plans*. Federal Register 68, no. 247 (December 24, 2003): 74483–91. United States, Department of State. "China — 25th Anniversary of Diplomatic Relations," press statement, December 31, 2003. http://www.state.gov/r/pa/prs/ps/2003/27632.htm.

Software	First note	[99] *Stata 8* (for Linux 64) (College Station, TX: Stata, 2003). [99] *Dreamweaver MX 2004* (San Francisco: Macromedia, 2003).
	Short note	[99] *Stata 8* (for Linux 64). [99] *Dreamweaver MX 2004*.
	Bibliography	*Stata 8* (for Linux 64). College Station, TX: Stata, 2003. *Dreamweaver MX 2004*. San Francisco: Macromedia, 2003.

Database	First note	[99] *Corpus Scriptorum Latinorum* database of Latin literature, http://www.forumromanum.org/literature/index.html. ▸ For a specific item within this database: [99] Gaius Julius Caesar, *Commentarii de bello civili*, ed. A. G. Peskett (Loeb Classical Library; London: W. Heinemann, 1914), in *Corpus Scriptorum Latinorum* database of Latin literature, http://www.thelatinlibrary.com/caes.html. [99] *Intellectual Property Treaties*, *InterAm Database* (Tucson, AZ: National Law Center for Inter-American Free Trade), http://www.natlaw.com/database.htm (accessed January 10, 2004). ▸ For a specific item within this database: [99] "Chile-U.S. Free Trade Agreement (June 6, 2003)," in *Intellectual Property Treaties*, *InterAm Database* (Tucson, AZ: National Law Center for Inter-American Free Trade), http://www.natlaw.com/treaties/chileusfta.htm (accessed January 12, 2004).
	Short note	[99] *Corpus Scriptorum Latinorum*. [99] *Intellectual Property Treaties*, *InterAm Database*. [99] "Chile-U.S. Free Trade Agreement."
	Bibliography	*Corpus Scriptorum Latinorum*. Database of Latin literature. http://www.forumromanum.org/literature/index.html. Caesar, Gaius Julius. *Commentarii de bello civili*, ed. A. G. Peskett. Loeb Classical Library. London: W. Heinemann, 1914. In *Corpus*

Database (*continued*)		*Scriptorum Latinorum* database of Latin literature. http://www.thelatinlibrary.com/caes.html.
		Intellectual Property Treaties, InterAm Database. Tucson, AZ: National Law Center for Inter-American Free Trade. http://www.natlaw.com/database.htm (accessed January 10, 2004).
		▸ For a specific item within the database:
		"Chile-U.S. Free Trade Agreement (June 6, 2003)." In *Intellectual Property Treaties, InterAm Database.* Tucson, AZ: National Law Center for Inter-American Free Trade. http://www.natlaw.com/treaties/chileusfta.htm (accessed January 12, 2004).

Web site, entire	First note	[99] Digital History Web site, ed. Steven Mintz, http://www.digitalhistory.uh.edu/index.cfm?.
		[99] Internet Public Library (IPL), http://www.ipl.org/.
		[99] Yale University, History Department home page, http://www.yale.edu/history/.
		▸ You may omit "home page" if it is obvious.
	Short note	[99] Digital History Web site.
		[99] Internet Public Library.
		[99] Yale History Department home page.
	Bibliography	Digital History Web site. Ed. Steven Mintz. http://www.digitalhistory.uh.edu/index.cfm?.
		Internet Public Library (IPL). http://www.ipl.org/.
		Yale University. History Department home page. http://www.yale.edu/history/.

Web page	First note	[99] Charles Lipson, "Scholarly Tools Online to Study World Politics," http://www.charleslipson.com/scholarly-links.htm.
	Short note	[99] Lipson, "Scholarly Tools."
	Bibliography	Lipson, Charles. "Scholarly Tools Online to Study World Politics." http://www.charleslipson.com/scholarly-links.htm.

▸ Include the title or description of the Web page if available. That way, if the link changes, it may still be possible to find the page through a search.

Weblog entries and comments

First note

⁹⁹ Daniel Drezner, "Blogger Weirdness," *Daniel W. Drezner* Weblog, entry posted December 30, 2003, http://www.danieldrezner.com/blog/ (accessed March 14, 2004).

⁹⁹ Tyler Cowen, "Trial by Jury," *Volokh Conspiracy* Weblog, entry posted December 30, 2003, http://volokh.com/ (accessed January 6, 2004).

⁹⁹ Kiwi (Janice Walker), "Citing Weblogs," *Kairosnews: A Weblog for Discussing Rhetoric, Technology, and Pedagogy*. Comment posted December 13, 2003, http://kairosnews.org/node/view/3542 (accessed December 28, 2003).

⁹⁹ Josh Chafetz, untitled Weblog entry, *OxBlog* Weblog, posted 12:06 p.m., December 27, 2003, http://oxblog.blogspot.com/ (accessed December 31, 2003).

Short note

⁹⁹ Drezner, "Blogger Weirdness."

⁹⁹ Cowen, "Trial by Jury."

⁹⁹ Kiwi (Janice Walker), "Citing Weblogs."

⁹⁹ Chafetz, untitled Weblog entry, December 27, 2003.

Bibliography

Drezner, Daniel. "Blogger Weirdness." *Daniel W. Drezner* Weblog. Entry posted December 30, 2003. http://www.danieldrezner.com/blog/ (accessed March 14, 2004).

Cowen, Tyler. "Trial by Jury." *Volokh Conspiracy* Weblog. Entry posted December 24, 2003. http://volokh.com/ (accessed January 6, 2004).

Kiwi (Janice Walker). "Citing Weblogs." *Kairosnews: A Weblog for Discussing Rhetoric, Technology, and Pedagogy*. Weblog comment posted December 13, 2003, to http://kairosnews.org/node/view/3542 (accessed December 28, 2003).

Chafetz, Josh. [Untitled Weblog entry.] *OxBlog*. Entry posted 12:06 p.m., December 27, 2003.

Weblog
entries and
comments
(*continued*)

http://oxblog.blogspot.com/ (accessed
December 31, 2003).

▸ Chafetz's posting had no title and is one of
several he posted the same day to this group
blog. Listing the time identifies it.

CHICAGO: CITATIONS TO TABLES AND NOTES	
CITATION	**REFERS TO**
106	page 106
106n	only note appearing on page 106
107n32	note number 32 on page 107, a page with several notes
89, table 6.2	table 6.2, which appears on page 89; similar for graphs and figures

CHICAGO: COMMON ABBREVIATIONS IN CITATIONS					
and others	et al.	editor	ed.	page	p.
appendix	app.	especially	esp.	pages	pp.
book	bk.	figure	fig.	part	pt.
chapter	chap.	note	n.	pseudonym	pseud.
compare	cf.	notes	nn.	translator	trans.
document	doc.	number	no.	versus	vs.
edition	ed.	opus	op.	volume	vol.

Note: All abbreviations are lowercase, followed by a period. Most form their plurals by adding "s." The exceptions are note (n. → nn.), opus (op. → opp.), page (p. → pp.), and translator (same abbreviation).

In citing poetry, do not use abbreviations for "line" or "lines" since a lowercase "l" is easily confused with the number one.

FAQS ABOUT CHICAGO-STYLE CITATIONS

Why do you put the state after some publishers and not after others?
The Chicago Manual of Style recommends using state names for all but the largest, best-known cities. To avoid confusion, they use Cambridge, MA, for Harvard and MIT Presses, but they use just Cambridge for Cambridge Uni-

versity Press in the ancient English university town. Also, you can drop the state name if it is already included in the publisher's title, such as Ann Arbor: University of Michigan Press.

What if a book is forthcoming?
Use "forthcoming" just as you would use the year.
   Here's a bibliographic entry:

Godot, Shlomo. *Still Waiting.* London: Verso, forthcoming.

What if the date or place of publication is missing?
Same idea as "forthcoming." Where you would normally put the date or place, use "n.d." (no date) or "n.p." (no place). For example: (Montreal, QC: McGill-Queen's University Press, n.d.)

What if the author is anonymous or not listed?
Usually, you omit the anonymous author and begin with the title.
   Since the bibliography is alphabetized by authors, what are you supposed to do when there is no author? Assume the title is the author, and don't count any initial articles such as "The." *The Chicago Manual of Style,* which has no listed authors, would be alphabetized under "C," after Broflovski and Cartman and before Crabtree.
   If, for some reason, the term "anonymous" is associated with the book and you want to include it, you can. List "Anonymous" as the author and alphabetize it. If you have several poems by unknown authors, you may wish to group them all under "Anonymous."
   If an author is technically anonymous but is actually known, put his name in brackets, as in [Johnson, Samuel] or [Madison, James] and list it wherever the author's name falls.

One book I cite has a title that ends with a question mark. Do I still put periods or commas after it?
No. If a title or subtitle ends with a question mark, don't add any additional punctuation. For example:

White, Eugene. "Was There a Solution to the *Ancien Régime*'s Financial Dilemma?" *Journal of Economic History* 49 (September 1989): 545–68.

When do I use "ibid."?
Use "ibid." if you are citing the same individual item you cited in the previous note, whether or not you are citing the same page. Ibid. is a Latin ab-

breviation meaning "in the same place." It is not italicized and refers only to one item. Here's an example, starting with note number 12:

[12] Hamby, *Man of the People*, 183.
[13] Ibid., 224.
[14] Ibid.
[15] Ibid., 53–55; Ferrell, *Harry S. Truman.*
[16] Hamby, *Man of the People*, 187.

Because ibid. refers only to a single item, it cannot be used in note 16. It wouldn't be clear if it referred to Hamby or Ferrell, and it can't refer to both. If the page number is the same as the previous note, then you can omit the pagination, as note 14 does.

Other Latin abbreviations, such as "op. cit." and "loc. cit.", were once used in footnotes but no longer are. Mirabile dictu.

Having said all this, I rarely use "ibid." myself. That's because I edit my text a lot. As I cut and paste, I move sentences around, and the citations move with them. If I used "ibid.," then I would need to retype some of the citations — and probably have to do it again after I reedit the text. What was once a time-saving device in the age of typewriters — after all, it's a lot easier to type "ibid." than to type a whole note — is now just a time-wasting device in the age of computers. So I dispense with it, at least until the paper is published.

Are notes single-spaced or double-spaced? What about the bibliography?

Space your footnotes and endnotes the same way you do your text.

As for your bibliography, I think it is easiest to read them if you single space within entries and put a double space between the entries. But check your department's requirements. They may require double spacing for everything.

I'm reading Mark Twain. Do I cite Twain or Samuel Clemens?

When pseudonyms are well known such as Mark Twain or Mother Teresa, you can use them alone, without explanation, if you wish.

If you want to include both the pseudonym and the given name, the rule is simple. Put the better-known name first, followed by the lesser-known one in brackets. It doesn't matter if the "real" name is the lesser-known one.

George Eliot [Mary Ann Evans]
Isak Dinesen [Karen Christence Dinesen, Baroness Blixen-Finecke]

Le Corbusier [Charles-Edouard Jeanneret]
Benjamin Disraeli [Lord Beaconsfield]
Lord Palmerston [Henry John Temple]
Krusty the Clown [Herschel S. Krustofski]

If you wish to include the pseudonym in a bibliographic entry, it reads:

Aleichem, Sholom [Solomon Rabinovitz]. *Fiddler on the Roof.* . . .

When I reference a Web site, should I include the date I accessed it?

Some citation styles say you should *always* list the access date. *The Chicago Manual of Style* recommends listing them only if they are relevant or if a particular discipline requires it. For example, include the access dates for Web sites that change often or display time-sensitive data. Even if the site does not change frequently, it's always okay to include the access date.

Be sure to write down the access date when you take notes. You might need to include it later.

6

MLA CITATIONS FOR
THE HUMANITIES

• • • • • • • • • • • • • •

The Modern Language Association (MLA) has developed a citation style that is widely used in the humanities. Instead of footnotes or endnotes, it uses in-text citations such as (Strier 125). Full information about each item appears in the bibliography, which MLA calls "Works Cited." Like other bibliographies, it contains three essential nuggets of information about each item: the author, title, and publication data. To illustrate, let's use a book by Fouad Ajami. The full entry in the Works Cited is

> Ajami, Fouad. The Dream Palace of the Arabs: A Generation's Odyssey. New York: Pantheon, 1998.

Titles are underlined rather than italicized.

In-text citations are brief and simple. To cite the entire book, just insert (Ajami) at the end of the sentence, or (Ajami 12) to refer to page 12. If your paper happens to cite several books by Ajami, be sure your reader knows which one you are referring to. If that's not clear in the sentence, then include a very brief title: (Ajami, Dream 12).

MLA citations can be even briefer — and they should be, whenever possible. They can omit the author and the title as long as it's clear which work is being cited. For example:

> As Ajami notes, these are long-standing problems in Arab intellectual life (14–33).

You can omit the in-text reference entirely if the author and title are clear and you are not citing specific pages. For instance:

> Gibbon's Decline and Fall of the Roman Empire established new standards of documentary evidence for historians.

In this case, there's nothing to put in an in-text reference that isn't already in the sentence. So, given MLA's consistent emphasis on brevity, you simply skip the reference. You still include Gibbon in your list of Works Cited.

Because in-text references are so brief, you can string several together in one parenthesis: (Bevington 17; Bloom 75; Vendler 51). The authors' names are separated by semicolons.

If Ajami's book were a three-volume work, then the citation to volume 3, page 17, would be (Ajami 3: 17). If you need to differentiate this work from others by the same author, then include the title: (Ajami, Dream 3: 17). If you wanted to cite the volume but not a specific page, then use (Ajami, vol. 3) or (Ajami, Dream, vol. 3). Why include "vol." here? So readers won't think you are citing page 3 of a one-volume work.

If several authors have the same last name, simply add their first initials to differentiate them: (C. Brontë, Jane Eyre), (E. Brontë, Wuthering Heights). Of course, full information about the authors and their works appears at the end, in the Works Cited.

Books like *Jane Eyre* appear in countless editions, and your readers may wish to look up passages in theirs. To make that easier, the MLA recommends that you add some information after the normal page citation. You might say, for example, that the passage appears in chapter 1. For poems, you would note the verse and lines.

Let's say that you quoted a passage from the first chapter of *Jane Eyre*, which appeared on page 7 in the edition you are using. Insert a semicolon after the page and add the chapter number, using a lowercase abbreviation for chapter: (E. Brontë, Wuthering Heights 7; ch. 1). For plays, the act, scene, and lines are separated by periods (Romeo and Juliet 1.3.12–15).

When you refer to online documents, there are often no pages to cite. As a substitute, include a section or paragraph number, if there is one. Just put a comma after the author's name, then list the section or paragraph: (Padgett, sec. 9.7) or (Snidal, pars. 12–18). If there's no numbering system, just list the author. Don't cite your printout because those pages vary from person to person, printer to printer.[1]

In-text citations normally appear at the end of sentences and are followed by the punctuation for the sentence itself. To illustrate:

---

1. These recommendations follow the MLA's own recommendation. MLA, "Frequently Asked Questions about MLA Style," http://www.mla.org/publications/style/style_faq/style_faq7.

A full discussion of these citation issues appears in the MLA Handbook (Gibaldi).

In this style, you can still use regular footnotes or endnotes for limited purposes. They can *only* be used for commentary, however, not for citations. If you need to cite some materials within the note itself, use in-text citations there, just as you would in the text.

For brevity — a paramount virtue of the MLA system — the names of publishers are also compressed: Princeton University Press becomes Princeton UP, the University of Chicago Press becomes U of Chicago P. For the same reason, most month names are abbreviated.

MLA throws brevity overboard, however, when referencing electronic information. If the works were originally printed, the Works Cited include all the print information, plus some extra information about the online versions, including Web sites, sponsoring organizations, access dates, and URLs. Of all citation styles, only MLA requires listing the sponsoring organization. This leads to redundancy. You are supposed to write: Encyclopaedia Britannica Online. 2004. Encyclopaedia Britannica . . . . Or CBSNews.com. 5 Jan. 2004. CBS . . . . The underlined titles are the works cited; the repeated name is the sponsoring organization. Actually, we'll see the name a third time in the URL, <http://www.cbs.com>. This seems like overkill to me, at least when the sponsoring organization is evident. But that's the current MLA style.

If an item is exclusively online, like a Web page or Weblog, the citation includes the author, the title of the Web page or site, the date it was created (or updated), plus information about the Web site, sponsoring organization, the date it was accessed, and the URL. It makes for a long list.

I have provided detailed information and examples in a table below. Because MLA style is often used in the humanities, where citations to plays, poems, paintings, and films are common, I include all of them. If you want still more examples or less common items, consult two useful books published by the MLA:

- Joseph Gibaldi, *MLA Style Manual and Guide to Scholarly Publishing*, 2nd ed. New York: Modern Language Association of America, 1998, 149–254.
- Joseph Gibaldi, *MLA Handbook for Writers of Research Papers*, 6th ed. New York: Modern Language Association of America, 2003.

They should be available in your library's reference section.

To make it easy to find the MLA citations you need, I've listed them here alphabetically, along with the pages where they are described.

MLA: IN-TEXT NOTES AND WORKS CITED

Book, one author	Works Cited	Lipson, Charles. <u>Reliable Partners: How Democracies Have Made a Separate Peace.</u> Princeton: Princeton UP, 2003. Reed, Christopher A. <u>Gutenberg in Shanghai: Chinese Print Capitalism, 1876–1937.</u> Vancouver: U British Columbia P, 2004. ▸ MLA style omits the publisher's state or province.
	In-text	(Lipson, <u>Reliable</u> 22–23) or (Lipson 22–23) or (22–23) ▸ Refers to pages 22–23. (Reed, <u>Gutenberg</u> 136) or (Reed 136) or (136)
Books, several by same author	Works Cited	Weinberg, Gerhard L. <u>Germany, Hitler, and World War II: Essays in Modern German and World History.</u> Cambridge: Cambridge UP, 1995. ———. <u>A World at Arms: A Global History of World War II.</u> Cambridge: Cambridge UP, 1994. ▸ The repetition of the author's name uses three hyphens, followed by a period.
	In-text	(Weinberg, <u>Germany</u> 34; Weinberg, <u>World</u> 456)
Book, multiple authors	Works Cited	Binder, Guyora, and Robert Weisberg. <u>Literary Criticisms of Law.</u> Princeton: Princeton UP, 2000. ▸ If four or more authors: Binder, Guyora, et al.
	In-text	(Binder and Weisberg, <u>Literary Criticisms</u> 15–26) or (Binder and Weisberg 15–26)
Book, multiple editions	Works Cited	Strunk, William, Jr., and E. B. White. <u>The Elements of Style.</u> 4th ed. New York: Longman, 2000. ▸ If this were a multivolume work, then the volume number would come after the edition: 4th ed. Vol. 2.
	In-text	(Strunk and White, <u>Elements</u> 12) or (Strunk and White 12)

Book, edited	Works Cited	Robinson, Francis, ed. <u>Cambridge Illustrated</u> <u>History of the Islamic World</u>. Cambridge: Cambridge UP, 1996. Gallagher, Kathleen, and David Booth, eds. <u>How</u> <u>Theatre Educates: Convergences and</u> <u>Counterpoints with Artists, Scholars, and</u> <u>Advocates</u>. Toronto: U Toronto P, 2003.
	In-text	(Robinson) (Gallagher and Booth)

Book, online	Works Cited	Dickens, Charles. <u>Great Expectations</u>. 1860–61. <u>Project Gutenberg Archive</u>. Etext 1400. 14 Jan. 2004 ‹http://www.gutenberg.net/etext98/ grexp10.txt›. ▸ The date when you access the online content (in this case, 14 Jan. 2004) comes immediately before the URL. Notice that the day comes before the month; that's standard with MLA. There is no punctuation between this date and the URL.[2]
	In-text	(Dickens) ▸ Since this electronic version does not have pagination, cite the chapter numbers. (Dickens, ch. 2)

Multivolume work	Works Cited	Pflanze, Otto. <u>Bismarck and the Development of</u> <u>Germany</u>. 3 vols. Princeton: Princeton UP, 1963–90.
	In-text	(Pflanze) or (Pflanze 3: 21) ▸ This refers to volume 3, page 21. (Pflanze, vol. 3) ▸ When a volume is referenced without a specific page, then use "vol." so the volume won't be confused for a page number.

---

2. This follows the MLA's most recent recommendation. Http://www.mla.org/ publications/style/style_faq/style_faq4.

Single volume in multivolume work	Works Cited	Pflanze, Otto. The Period of Fortification, 1880–1898. Princeton: Princeton UP, 1990. Vol. 3 of Bismarck and the Development of Germany. 3 vols. 1963–90. Iriye, Akira. The Globalizing of America. Cambridge: Cambridge University Press, 1993. Vol. 3 of Cambridge History of American Foreign Relations, ed. Warren I. Cohen, 4 vols. 1993.
	In-text	(Pflanze) (Iriye)

Reprint of earlier edition	Works Cited	Barzun, Jacques. Simple and Direct: A Rhetoric for Writers. 1985. Chicago: U of Chicago P, 1994. Smith, Adam. An Inquiry into the Nature and Causes of the Wealth of Nations. 1776. Ed. Edwin Cannan. Chicago: U of Chicago P, 1976.
	In-text	(Barzun, Simple) or (Barzun) (Smith, Wealth of Nations) or (Smith)

Translated volume	Works Cited	Weber, Max. The Protestant Ethic and the Spirit of Capitalism. 1904–5. Trans. Talcott Parsons. New York: Charles Scribner's Sons, 1958. Tocqueville, Alexis de. Democracy in America. Ed. J. P. Mayer. Trans. George Lawrence. New York: HarperCollins, 2000.
		▸ Editor and translator are listed in the order they appear on the book's title page.
		Beowulf: A New Verse Translation. Trans. Seamus Heaney. New York: Farrar, Straus and Giroux, 2000.
		▸ *Beowulf* is an anonymous poem. The translator's name normally comes after the title. But there is an exception. If you wish to comment on the translator's work, then place the translator's name first. For example:
		Seamus Heaney, trans. Beowulf: A New Verse Translation. New York: Farrar, Straus and Giroux, 2000.

Parsons, Talcott, trans. The Protestant Ethic and the Spirit of Capitalism, by Max Weber. 1904–5. New York: Charles Scribner's Sons, 1958.

In-text

(Weber, Protestant Ethic) or (Weber)
(Tocqueville, Democracy in America) or (Tocqueville)
(Heaney, Beowulf) or (Beowulf)
(Parsons)

Chapter in edited book | Works Cited | Keohane, Robert. "The Demand for International Regimes." In International Regimes, ed. Stephen Krasner. Ithaca: Cornell UP, 1983. 56–67.

In-text

(Keohane 56–67)

Journal article | Works Cited | Kleppinger, Stanley V. "On the Influence of Jazz Rhythm in the Music of Aaron Copland." American Music 21.1 (Spring 2003): 74–111.
- Refers to volume 21, number 1.
- The issue number is optional if it is clear how to find the article (perhaps because you have already included the month or because the pages run continuously through the year). But if each issue begins with page 1 and you include only the year, then you need to add the issue number or month to show where the article appears: American Music 21.1 (2003): 74–111.

In-text

(Kleppinger) or (Kleppinger 74–82) or (Kleppinger, "Aaron Copland" 74–82)
- The title may be needed to differentiate this article from others by the same author.

Journal article, multiple authors | Works Cited | Koremenos, Barbara, Charles Lipson, and Duncan Snidal. "The Rational Design of International Institutions." International Organization 55 (Autumn 2001): 761–99.
- If there are four or more authors: Koremenos, Barbara, et al.

In-text

(Koremenos, Lipson, and Snidal 761–99)

Journal article online	Works Cited	Small, Christopher. "Why Doesn't the Whole World Love Chamber Music?" American Music 19.3 (Autumn 2001): 340–59. JSTOR 15 Mar. 2004 ‹http://www.jstor.org/search›.
		▸ This is a normal print journal, available online from multiple sources, with the same pagination as the print version. Here I list it through JSTOR. The URL is quite long, so MLA recommends listing only the search page.
		North, Dan. "Magic and Illusion in Early Cinema." Studies in French Cinema 1.2 (2001): 70–79. EBSCOhost Research Database 6 Jan. 2004 ‹http://search.epnet.com›.
	In-text	(Small) or (Small 341–43) or (Small, "Chamber Music" 341–43)
		(North) or (North 70–79) or (North, "Magic" 70–79)
Newspaper or magazine article, no author	Works Cited	"Report of 9/11 Panel Cites Lapses by C.I.A. and F.B.I." New York Times 23 July 2003: 1.
		▸ This refers to page 1.
	In-text	("Report of 9/11 Panel" 1)
Newspaper or magazine article with author	Works Cited	Bruni, Frank. "Pope Pleads for End to Terrorism and War." New York Times 26 Dec. 2003, national ed.: A21.
		▸ It's always fine to include the headline and reporter's name. The MLA says you can omit them, though, if they do not add to the point you are making in the text.
	In-text	(Bruni A21)
Newspaper or magazine article online	Works Cited	"European Unity: The History of an Idea." The Economist 30 Dec. 2003. 6 Jan. 2004 ‹http://www.economist.com/world/europe/displayStory.cfm?story_id=2313040›.
		▸ The first date refers to the article, the second to the day it was accessed.

▸ For magazines and newspapers, there is no need
to reference the sponsoring organization.

Salamon, Julie. "Collaborating on the Future at
the Modern." New York Times 26 Dec. 2003.
2 Jan. 2004 ‹http://www.nytimes.com/2003/
12/26/arts/design/26CURA.html›.

In-text

("European Unity")
(Salamon) or (Salamon, "Collaborating") if you
cite more than one article by this author.

Review   Works Cited

Orr, H. Allen. "What's Not in Your Genes." Rev. of
Nature via Nurture: Genes, Experience, and
What Makes Us Human, by Matt Ridley. New
York Review of Books 50 (14 Aug. 2003): 38–
40.

In-text   (Orr) or (Orr, "Genes")

Unpublished   Works Cited
paper,
thesis, or
dissertation

Nishi, Takayushi. "The Humiliating Gift: Negative
Reactions to International Help." Paper
presented at the Program on International
Politics, Economics, and Security, U Chicago.
4 Mar. 2004.

Besser-Jones, Lorraine. "The Moral Commitment
to Public Reason." MA thesis. Claremont
Graduate School, 1997.

Pérez-Torres, Rafael. "Screen Play and Inscription:
Narrative Strategies in Four Post-1960s
Novels." Diss. Stanford, 1989.

In-text

(Nishi 1–35)
(Besser-Jones)
(Pérez-Torres)

Microfilm,   Works Cited
microfiche

Abbott, Alice Irving. Circumstantial Evidence.
New York: W. B. Smith, 1882. In American
Fiction, 1774–1910. Reel A-1. Woodbridge:
Gale/Primary Source Microfilm, 1998.

King, Martin Luther, Jr., FBI file [microform]. Ed.
David J. Garrow. 16 reels. Frederick:
U Publications of Am, 1984.

Microfilm, microfiche (*continued*)	In-text	(Abbott) To cite page 13 on reel A-1, use (Abbott A-1: 13) (King) To cite reel 2, page 12, use (King 2: 12)

Encyclopedia, hard copy and online	Works Cited	"African Arts." <u>Encyclopaedia Britannica</u>. 15th ed. 1987. 13: 134–80. ▸ Alphabetize by the first significant word in title. ▸ Volume and page numbers are optional. ▸ Edition and year are required, but you can omit the city and publisher for well-known encyclopedias, dictionaries, and other references. "Art, African." <u>Encyclopaedia Britannica Online</u>. 2004. Encyclopaedia Britannica. 5 Jan. 2004 ‹http://search.eb.com/eb/article?eu=119483›. ▸ Why does the name, *Encyclopaedia Britannica*, appear twice? Because it is both the publication and the "sponsoring organization," and MLA rules currently require that you list both. Chanda, Jacqueline. "African Art and Architecture," <u>Microsoft Encarta Online Encyclopedia</u>. 2004. Microsoft Corporation. 7 Jan. 2004 ‹http://encarta.msn.com/encyclopedia_761574805/African_Art.html›.
	In-text	("African Arts" 13: 137) (Chanda)

Reference book, hard copy and online	Works Cited	Pendergast, Sara, and Tom Pendergast, eds. <u>Reference Guide to World Literature</u>. 3rd ed. 2 vols. Detroit: St. James Press/Thomson-Gale, 2003. Cannon, John, ed. <u>Oxford Companion to British History</u>. New York: Oxford University Press, 2002. ‹http://www.oxfordreference.com/views/BOOK_SEARCH.html?book=t110&subject=s11›. Cicioni, Mirna, "The periodic table (Il sistema periodico), prose by Primo Levi, 1975." <u>Reference Guide to World Literature</u>. Ed. Sara Pendergast and Tom Pendergast. 3rd ed. 2 vols. Detroit: St. James Press/Thomson-Gale, 2003. 2: 1447.

"Polytheism." The New Dictionary of Cultural
   Literacy. Ed. E. D. Hirsch Jr., Joseph F. Kett,
   and James Trefil. 3rd ed. Boston: Houghton
   Mifflin, 2002. 2 Feb. 2004 ‹http://www
   .bartleby.com/59/5/polytheism.html›.
   ▸ This is a hard-copy book that is also available
      online.
"Napoleon I." The Biographical Dictionary. 2004.
   S-9 Technologies. 5 Jan. 2004 ‹http://www.s9
   .com/biography/search.html›

In-text   (Pendergast and Pendergast)
           (Cannon)
           (Cicioni 2: 1447)
           ("Polytheism")
           ("Napoleon I")

Dictionary,   Works Cited   "Historiography." Merriam-Webster's Collegiate
hard copy,   Dictionary. 11th ed. 2003.
online, and   ▸ You can omit the publisher information.
CD-ROM   "Protest, *v.*" Compact Edition of the Oxford
                               English Dictionary. 1971 ed. II: 2335.
                               ▸ The word "protest" is both a noun and a verb,
                                  and I am citing the verb here.
                            "Pluck, *n.*" Def. 1. *Oxford English Dictionary*. Ed.
                               J. A. Simpson and E. S. C. Weiner. 2nd ed.
                               Oxford: Clarendon Press, 1989. Oxford
                               University Press. 5 Jan. 2004 ‹http://
                               dictionary.oed.com/cgi/entry/00181836›.
                               ▸ There are two separate entries for the noun
                                  pluck, and I am citing the first, hence *n*. Def. 1.
                                  The second is for an obscure fish.
                            "Balustrade." Microsoft Encarta Online Dictionary.
                               2004. Microsoft. 5 Jan. 2004 ‹http://encarta
                               .msn.com/dictionary_/balustrade.html›.
                            "Citation." American Heritage Dictionary of the
                               English Language. 4th ed. CD-ROM. Boston:
                               Houghton Mifflin, 2000.

              In-text   ("Protest" II: 2335)
                           (Compact OED II: 2335)
                           ("Citation") or (American Heritage Dictionary)

Bible	Works Cited	*Tanakh: The Holy Scriptures: The New JPS Translation According to the Traditional Hebrew Text.* Philadelphia: Jewish Publication Society, 1985.
		▸ The Bible does *not* usually appear in Works Cited, although you can include it if you wish to cite a particular version or translation.
	In-text	**Genesis 1.1, 1.3–5, 2.4.**
		▸ Books may be abbreviated, such as Gen. 1.1, 1.3–5, 2.4.
		▸ Abbreviations for the next four books are Ex., Lev., Num., and Deut. Abbreviations for other books are easily found with a Web search for "abbreviations + Bible."

Speech, academic talk, or course lecture	Works Cited	Ferrell, Will. "Class Day Speech." Speech at Harvard. Cambridge, MA. 4 June 2003.
		Kamhi, Michelle. "Rescuing Art from 'Visual Culture.'" Speech to annual convention of the National Art Education Association. Minneapolis, MN. 7 Apr. 2003.
		Doniger, Wendy. Course lecture. University of Chicago. Chicago, IL. 12 Mar. 2004.
		▸ Or, using a more descriptive name for an untitled lecture:
		Doniger, Wendy. Course lecture on evil in Hindu mythology. University of Chicago. Chicago, IL. 12 Mar. 2004.
	In-text	(Ferrell)
		(Kamhi)
		(Doniger)

Interview: personal, telephone, or in print	Works Cited	King, Coretta Scott. Personal interview. 14 Jan. 2004.
		Wiesel, Elie. Telephone interview. 16 Feb. 2004.
		Arroyo, Gloria Macapagal. "A Time for Prayer." Interview with Michael Schuman. *Time.* 28 July 2003. 13 Jan. 2004 <http://www.time.com/time/nation/article/0,8599,471205,00.html>.
	In-text	(King)

Poem	Works Cited	Bishop, Elizabeth. "The Fish." The Complete Poems, 1927–1979. New York: Noonday Press/Farrar, Straus and Giroux, 1983. 42–44. Lowell, Robert. "For the Union Dead." The Top 500 Poems. Ed. William Harmon. New York: Columbia University Press, 1992. 1061–63.
	In-text	(Bishop 42–44) or (Bishop, "The Fish" 42–44) or ("The Fish" 42–44) or (42–44) ▸ For poems such as "The Fish," you can note the verse and lines separated by periods or state (lines 10–12). (Lowell 1061–63) or (Lowell, "Union Dead" 1061–63)
Play	Works Cited	Shakespeare, Romeo and Juliet. ▸ If you wish to cite a specific edition, then: Shakespeare, Romeo and Juliet. Ed. Brian Gibbons. London: Methuen, 1980.
	In-text	(Shakespeare, Romeo and Juliet 1.3.12–15) or (Romeo and Juliet 1.3.12–15) or (1.3.12–15) if the play's name is clear in the text. ▸ This refers to act 1, scene 3, lines 12–15 (separated by periods).
Performance of play or dance	Works Cited	Kiss. Chor. Susan Marshall. Music Arvo Pärt. Perf. Cheryl Mann, Tobin Del Cuore. Hubbard Street Dance Chicago. Joan W. and Irving B. Harris Theater for Music and Dance, Chicago. Mar. 12, 2004. Topdog/Underdog. By Suzan Lori-Parks. Dir. Amy Morton. Perf. K. Todd Freeman, David Rainey. Steppenwolf Theater, Chicago. 2 Nov. 2003. ▸ If you are concentrating on one person's work in theater, music, dance, or other collaborative arts, put that person's name first. For example, if you are focusing on David Rainey's acting: Rainey, David, perf. Topdog/Underdog. By Suzan Lori-Parks. Dir. Amy Morton . . . . ▸ If, by contrast, you are focusing on Amy Morton's directing or on directing in general:

Performance of play or dance (*continued*)		Morton, Amy, dir. Topdog/Underdog. By Suzan Lori-Parks. Perf. David Rainey . . . .
	In-text	(Kiss)
		(Topdog/Underdog) or (Rainey) or (Morton)
Television program	Works Cited	"Bart vs. Lisa vs. 3rd Grade." The Simpsons. Writ. T. Long. Dir. S. Moore. Episode: 1403 F55079. Fox. 17 Nov. 2002.
	In-text	("Bart vs. Lisa")
Film	Works Cited	Godfather II. Dir. Francis Ford Coppola. Perf. Al Pacino, Robert De Niro, Robert Duvall, Diane Keaton. Screenplay Francis Ford Coppola and Mario Puzo based on the novel by Mario Puzo. Paramount Pictures, 1974. DVD. Paramount Home Video, Godfather DVD Collection, 2003. ▸ Required: title, director, studio, and year released. Michael Corleone insists. ▸ Optional: actors, producers, screenwriters, editors, cinematographers, and other information. Include what you need for analysis in your paper, in order of their importance to your analysis. Their names appear between the title and the distributor. ▸ If you are concentrating on one person's work, put that person's name and role (such as performer) first, before the title: Coppola, Francis Ford, dir. Godfather II. Perf. Al Pacino, Robert De Niro, Robert Duvall, Diane Keaton. Paramount Pictures, 1974. DVD. Paramount Home Video, Godfather DVD Collection, 2003.
	In-text	(Godfather II)
Artwork, original	Works Cited	Tintoretto, Jacopo Robusti. The Birth of John the Baptist. 1550s. Oil on canvas, 181 x 266 cm. Hermitage, St. Petersburg. ▸ Year, size, and medium are optional.

	In-text	(Tintoretto) or (Tintoretto, <u>Birth of John the Baptist</u>)
Artwork, reproduction	Works Cited	Tintoretto, Jacopo Robusti. <u>The Birth of John the Baptist</u>. 1550s. Hermitage, St. Petersburg. In <u>Tintoretto: Tradition and Identity</u>. By Tom Nichols. London: Reaktion Books, 1999. 47.
	In-text	(Tintoretto) or (Tintoretto, <u>Birth of John the Baptist</u>)
Artwork, online	Works Cited	Tintoretto, Jacopo Robusti. <u>The Birth of John the Baptist</u>. 1550s. Hermitage, St. Petersburg. State Hermitage Museum. 5 Jan. 2004 ‹http://www.hermitage.ru/html_En/index.html›.
		Tintoretto, Jacopo Robusti. <u>The Birth of John the Baptist</u> (detail). 1550s. Hermitage, St. Petersburg. CGFA-Virtual Art Museum. 5 Jan. 2004 ‹http://cgfa.floridaimaging.com/t/p-tintore1.htm›.
		▸ The same artwork accessed through the museum's site and another site. Note that the sponsors of the different Web sites are listed, as well as their URLs.
	In-text	(Tintoretto) or (Tintoretto, <u>Birth of John the Baptist</u>)
Photograph	Works Cited	Adams, Ansel. <u>Monolith, the Face of Half Dome, Yosemite National Park</u>. 1927. Art Institute, Chicago.
	In-text	(Adams) or (Adams, <u>Monolith</u>)
Musical recording	Works Cited	Johnson, Robert. "Come on in My Kitchen (Take 1)." Rec. 23 Nov. 1936. <u>Robert Johnson: King of the Delta Blues Singers</u>. Expanded edition. Columbia/Legacy, CK 65746, 1998.
		Allman Brothers Band. "Come on in My Kitchen." By Robert Johnson. <u>Shades of Two Worlds</u>. Sony, 1991.

Musical recording (*continued*)		Barber, Samuel. "Cello Sonata, for cello and piano, Op. 6." <u>Barber: Adagio for Strings, Violin Concerto, Orchestral and Chamber Works</u>. Disc 2. St. Louis Symphony. Cond. Leonard Slatkin. Cello, Alan Stepansky. Piano, Israela Margalit. EMI Classics 74287, 2001.

▶ The catalog numbers are optional but helpful.

▶ There is no need to say that a recording is on CD. However, if it is on cassette, LP, or some other medium, that should be listed just before the publisher. For example:

Holloway, Stanley. "Get Me to the Church on Time." <u>My Fair Lady, Original London Cast Recording</u>. Book and lyrics, Alan Jay Lerner. Music, Frederick Loewe. Rec. 1958. Audiocassette. Broadway/Legacy 060539, 1998.

▶ If you are concentrating on one person's work, such as the pianist, her name can come first:

Margalit, Israela, piano. "Cello Sonata, for cello and piano, Op. 6." <u>Barber: Adagio for Strings, Violin Concerto, Orchestral and Chamber Works</u>. Disc 2. St. Louis Symphony. Cond. Leonard Slatkin. Cello, Alan Stepansky. EMI Classics 74287, 2001.

	In-text	(Johnson) or (Johnson, "Come on in My Kitchen") (Allman Brothers) or (Allman Brothers, "Come on in My Kitchen") (Holloway) or (Holloway, "Get Me to the Church on Time") (Margalit) or (Margalit, "Cello Sonata")

Sheet music	Works Cited	Bach, Johann Sebastian. <u>Toccata and Fugue in D Minor</u>. 1708. BWV 565. Arr. Ferruccio Benvenuto Busoni for solo piano. New York: G. Schirmer LB1629, 1942.

▶ This piece was written in 1708 and has the standard Bach classification BWV 565. The arrangement is published by G. Schirmer, with their catalog number LB1629.

	In-text	(Toccata and Fugue in D Minor) or (Bach, Toccata and Fugue in D Minor)
Liner notes	Works Cited	Reich, Steven. Liner notes. Different Trains. Kronos Quartet. Elektra/Nonesuch 9 79176-2, 1988.
	In-text	(Reich, Different Trains)
Government document, hard copy and online	Works Cited	Cong. Rec. 23 July 2003: 2468–72. United States. Cong. Senate. Committee on Armed Services. Hearings on S. 758, A Bill to Promote the National Security by Providing for a National Defense Establishment. 80th Cong., 1st sess., 1947. Freedman, Stephen. Four-Year Impacts of Ten Programs on Employment Stability and Earnings Growth. The National Evaluation of Welfare-to-Work Strategies. Washington, DC: U.S. Department of Education. 2000. ERIC Document Reproduction Service No. ED450262. United States. Department of State. China — 25th Anniversary of Diplomatic Relations. Press Statement. 31 Dec. 2003. 5 Jan. 2004 <http://www.state.gov/r/pa/prs/ps/2003/27632.htm>.
	In-text	(U.S. Cong., Senate, Committee on Armed Services) ▸ If you are only referencing one item from that committee, then in-text citations don't need to include the hearing number or report. (U.S. Cong., Senate, Committee on Armed Services, Hearings on S. 758, 1947) ▸ If you refer to several items from the committee, indicate which one you are citing. You can shorten that after the first use: (Hearings on S. 758). (Freedman) or (Freedman, Four-Year Impacts) (U.S. Department of State)

Database	Works Cited	Internet Movie Database (IMDb). 2004. Internet Movie Database. 6 Jan. 2004 ‹http://www.imdb.com/›.
		Corpus Scriptorum Latinorum database of Latin literature. 2003. Forum Romanum. 5 Jan. 2004 ‹http://www.forumromanum.org/literature/index.html›.
		▸ For a specific item within this database:
		Caesar, Gaius Julius. Commentarii de bello civili. Ed. A. G. Peskett. Loeb Classical Library. London: W. Heinemann, 1914. Corpus Scriptorum Latinorum database of Latin literature. 2003. Forum Romanum. 5 Jan. 2004 ‹http://www.thelatinlibrary.com/caes.html›.
	In-text	(IMDb)
		(Corpus Scriptorum Latinorum)
		(Gaius Julius Caesar) or (Gaius Julius Caesar, Commentarii de bello civili)
Software	Works Cited	Dreamweaver MX 2004. San Francisco: Macromedia, 2003.
	In-text	(Dreamweaver MX 2004)
Web site, entire	Works Cited	Digital History. Ed. Steven Mintz. 2003. U of Houston et al. 6 Jan. 2004. ‹http://www.digitalhistory.uh.edu/ index.cfm?›.
		Internet Public Library (IPL). 2004. School of Information, University of Michigan. 7 Jan. 2004 ‹http://www.ipl.org/›.
	In-text	(Internet Public Library) or (IPL)
Web page	Works Cited	Lipson, Charles. "Advice on Getting a Great Recommendation." Web page. 2003. 6 Jan. 2004 ‹http://www.charleslipson.com/courses/Getting-a-good-recommendation.htm›.
		▸ If the URL takes up more than one line, break *after* a single or double slash and *before* a period, a comma, a hyphen, an underline, or a number sign.

> ‣ MLA currently suggests listing the date when you accessed a particular Web file. *The Chicago Manual of Style* now recommends against it, unless there is a reason.

In-text

(Lipson) or (Lipson, "Advice")

> ‣ Web pages and other online documents may not have pages. You may, however, be able to cite to a specific section (Lipson, sec. 7) or paragraph (Lipson, pars. 3–5).

Weblog, entries and comments

Works Cited

Jerz, Dennis. "How to Cite a Weblog and Weblog Comments in MLA Style." Weblog entry. 11 Dec. 2003. Kairosnews: A Weblog for Discussing Rhetoric, Technology, and Pedagogy. 2 Jan. 2004 ‹http://kairosnews .org/node/ view/3542›.

Kiwi (Janice Walker). "Citing Weblogs." Weblog comment. 3 Dec. 2003. Kairosnews: A Weblog for Discussing Rhetoric, Technology, and Pedagogy. 3 Jan. 2004 ‹http://kairosnews .org/node/view/3542›.

Cowen, Tyler. "Trial by Jury." Weblog entry. 24 Dec. 2003 Volokh Conspiracy. 6 Jan. 2004 ‹http://volokh.com/›.

Chafetz, Josh. Untitled Weblog entry. 27 Dec. 2003, 12:06 p.m. OxBlog. 29 Dec. 2003 ‹http://oxblog.blogspot.com/›.

> ‣ Chafetz's posting had no title and is one of several he posted to this group blog on the same day. Listing the time identifies it.

In-text

(Jerz) or (Jerz, "How to Cite a Weblog")

MLA uses abbreviations frequently. Here are the most common:

MLA: COMMON ABBREVIATIONS IN WORKS CITED					
and others	et al.	especially	esp.	paragraph	par.
appendix	app.	figure	fig.	part	pt.
book	bk.	note	n	pseudonym	pseud.
chapter	ch. or chap.	notes	nn	translator	trans.
compare	cf.	number	no.	verse	v.
document	doc.	opus	op.	verses	vv.
edition	ed.	page	p.	versus	vs.
editor	ed.	pages	pp.	volume	vol.

All abbreviations are lowercase, followed by a period. Most form their plurals by adding "s." The exceptions are note (n → nn), opus (op. → opp.), page (p. → pp.), and translator (same abbreviation).

In citing poetry, do not use abbreviations for "line" or "lines" since a lowercase "l" is easily confused with the number one. Use either the full word, or, if the meaning is clear, simply the number.

FAQS ABOUT MLA CITATIONS

How do I handle the citation when one author quotes another?
That happens frequently, as in Donald Kagan's book *The Peloponnesian Wars*, which often quotes Thucydides. Using MLA style, you might write:

> Kagan approvingly quotes Thucydides, who says that Athens acquired this vital site "because of the hatred they already felt toward the Spartans" (qtd. in Kagan 14).

In the Works Cited, you include Kagan but *not* Thucydides.

Some MLA citations, such as newspaper articles, use the names of months. Which ones should I abbreviate and which ones should I spell out?
Use three-letter abbreviations for all but the short names: May, June, and July.

7

APA CITATIONS FOR THE SOCIAL SCIENCES, EDUCATION, ENGINEERING, AND BUSINESS

• • • • • • • • • • • • • •

APA citations are widely used in psychology, education, engineering, business, and the social sciences. Like MLA citations, they are in-text. They use notes only for analysis and commentary, not to cite references. Unlike MLA, however, APA emphasizes the date of publication, which comes immediately after the author's name. That's probably because as scholarship cumulates in the sciences and empirical social sciences (where APA is used), it is important to know whether the research was conducted recently and whether it came before or after other research. At least that's the rationale.

Detailed information on the APA system is available in

• *Publication Manual of the American Psychological Association.* 5th ed. Washington, DC: American Psychological Association, 2001.

Like the *Chicago Manual of Style* and MLA style books, the APA manual should be available in your library's reference section. For more details on engineering papers, you can also consult an online guide from the American Society of Civil Engineers, available at http://www.pubs.asce.org/authors/index.html#ref.

To get started, let's look at APA references for a journal article, a chapter in an edited book, and a book as they appear at the end of a paper. APA calls this a "Reference List." (MLA calls it "Works Cited," and Chicago calls it a "Bibliography.")

Lipson, C. (1991). Why are some international agreements informal? *International Organization, 45,* 495–538.

Lipson, C. (1994). Is the future of collective security like the past? In
G. Downs (Ed.), *Collective security beyond the cold war* (pp. 105–
131). Ann Arbor: University of Michigan Press.

Lipson, C. (2003). *Reliable partners: How democracies have made a
separate peace.* Princeton, NJ: Princeton University Press.

This list for the distinguished author C. Lipson follows another APA rule.
All entries for a single author are arranged by year of publication, beginning with the earliest. If there were two entries for a particular year, say
2004, they would be alphabetized by title and the first would be labeled
(2004a), the second (2004b). Also note the APA's rules for capitalizing book
and article titles. They are treated like sentences, with only the first words
capitalized. If there's a colon in the title, the first word after the colon is also
capitalized. Proper nouns are capitalized, of course, just as they are in sentences.

In these reference lists, single-author entries precede those with coauthors. So Pinker, S. (as a sole author) would proceed Pinker, S., & Jones, B.
In the APA system, multiple authors are joined by an ampersand "&" rather
than the word "and." It is not clear why. Just accept it as a rule, like how
many minutes are in a soccer game.

The authors' first names are always reduced to initials. Pagination is not
included for in-text references, except for direct quotes (where the pages are
preceded by "p." or "pp."). That makes it different from the other systems,
as does its frequent use of commas and parentheses.

When works are cited in the text, the citation includes the author's name,
for example (Wilson, 2004d), unless the author's name has already been
mentioned in that sentence. If the sentence includes the author's name, the
citation omits it. For instance:

Nye (2004) presents considerable data to back up his claims.

The examples in this chapter focus on the social sciences, education, engineering, and business, where APA citations are most widely used, just as
the MLA examples focus on the humanities, where that style is common.

To make it easy to find the APA citations you need, I've listed them here
alphabetically, along with the pages where they are described.

INDEX OF APA CITATIONS IN THIS CHAPTER

APA: IN-TEXT CITATIONS AND REFERENCE LIST

| Book, one author | Reference list | Mandelbaum, M. (2002). *The ideas that conquered the world: Peace, democracy and free markets in the twenty-first century.* New York: Public Affairs.
Lundy, C. (2003). *Social work and social justice: A structural approach to practice.* Peterborough, ON: Broadview Press.
▶ Canadian provinces are abbreviated with two letters. |
| | In-text | (Mandelbaum, 2002)
(Lundy, 2003) |

Books, several by same author	Reference list	Elster, J. (1989a). *The cement of society: A study of social order*. Cambridge: Cambridge University Press. Elster, J. (1989b). *Nuts and bolts for the social sciences*. Cambridge: Cambridge University Press. Elster, J. (1989c). *Solomonic judgements: Studies in the limitations of rationality*. Cambridge: Cambridge University Press; Paris: Editions de la Maison des sciences de l'homme. Elster, J., & Moene, K. O. (Eds.). (1989). *Alternatives to capitalism*. Cambridge: Cambridge University Press. ► Note that the author's name is repeated. APA does not use dashes for repetition. ► When the same author or coauthors have several publications in the same year, list them alphabetically (by the first significant word in the title). Label them as "a," "b," and "c." The last item by Elster is *not* labeled "d" because its authorship is different. ► Coauthored books like Elster & Moene follow a writer's single-author ones, in the alphabetical order of the second author's name.
	In-text	(Elster, 1989a, 1989b, 1989c; Elster & Moene, 1989)
Book, multiple authors	Reference list	Reiter, D., & Stam, A. C. (2002). *Democracies at war*. Princeton, NJ: Princeton University Press. ► Name the first six authors, then add "et al."
	In-text	(Reiter & Stam, 2002) ► For two to five authors, name all authors in the first citation. Beginning with the second reference, name only the first author, then add "et al." ► For six or more authors, name only the first author, then add "et al." for all citations. ► Use "&" within parenthetical references but not in the text itself.

Book, multiple editions	Reference list	Strunk, W., Jr., & White, E. B. (2000). *The elements of style* (4th ed.). New York: Longman. ► If it says "revised edition" rather than 4th edition, use (Rev. ed.) in the same spot.
	In-text	(Strunk & White, 2000) ► To refer to a specific page for a quotation: (Strunk & White, 2000, p. 12)
Book, multiple editions, no author	Reference list	*National Partnership for Immunization reference guide* (2nd ed.). (2003). Alexandria, VA: National Partnership for Immunization. *Publication manual of the American Psychological Association* (5th ed.). (2001). Washington, DC: American Psychological Association. ► For multiple editions without authors, the form is *Title* (18th ed.). (year). City, STATE: Publisher.
	In-text	(National Partnership for Immunization [NPI], 2003) ► Subsequent references are (NPI, 2003) (American Psychological Association [APA], 2001) ► Subsequent references are (APA, 2001)
Book, edited	Reference list	Shweder, R. A., Minow, M., & Markus, H. (Eds.). (2002). *Engaging cultural differences: The multicultural challenge in liberal democracies*. New York: Russell Sage Foundation Press. Katznelson, I., & Shefter, M. (Eds.). (2002). *Shaped by war and trade: International influences on American political development*. Princeton, NJ: Princeton University Press.
	In-text	(Shweder, Minow, & Markus, 2002) (Katznelson & Shefter, 2002)
Book, online	Reference list	Reed, J. (1922). *Ten days that shook the world*. Project Gutenberg. Etext 3076. Retrieved January 12, 2004, from ftp://ibiblio.org/pub/docs/books/gutenberg/etext02/10daz10.txt

Book, online (*continued*)		▶ APA does *not* put a period after the URL, making it different from most other reference styles.
	In-text	(Reed, 1922)
Multivolume work	Reference list	Pflanze, O. (1963–1990). *Bismarck and the development of Germany* (Vols. 1–3). Princeton, NJ: Princeton University Press.
	In-text	(Pflanze, 1963–1990)
Single volume in multivolume work	Reference list	Pflanze, O. (1990). *The period of fortification, 1880–1898: Vol. 3. Bismarck and the development of Germany.* Princeton, NJ: Princeton University Press.
	In-text	(Pflanze, 1990)
Reprint of earlier edition	Reference list	Smith, A. (1976). *An Inquiry into the nature and causes of the wealth of nations.* E. Cannan (Ed.). Chicago: University of Chicago Press. (Original work published 1776)
	In-text	(Smith, 1776/1976)
Translated volume	Reference list	Weber, M. (1958). *The Protestant ethic and the spirit of capitalism.* T. Parsons (Trans.). New York: Charles Scribner's Sons. (Original work published 1904–1905)
	In-text	(Weber, 1904–1905/1958)
Chapter in edited book	Reference list	Keohane, R. (1983). The demand for international regimes. In S. Krasner (Ed.), *International regimes* (pp. 56–67). Ithaca, NY: Cornell University Press.
	In-text	(Keohane, 1983)
Journal article	Reference list	Lipson, C. (1991). Why are some international agreements informal? *International organization, 45,* 495–538.

▸ Notice that article titles are not in quotes.

▸ The journal's volume number is italicized, but the issue number and pages are not. The word "volume" (or "vol.") is omitted.

▸ There's no need to name a specific issue if the journal pages are numbered continuously throughout the year. However, if each issue begins with page 1, then the issue's number or month is necessary to find the article: *45*(2), 15–30.

	In-text	(Lipson, 1991)

Journal article, multiple authors	Reference list	Koremenos, B., Lipson, C., & Snidal, D. (2001). The rational design of international institutions. *International Organization*, *55*, 761–799. Hansen, S. S., Munk-Jorgensen, P., Guldbaek, B., Solgard, T., Lauszus, K. S., Albrechtsen, N., et al. (2000). Psychoactive substance use diagnoses among psychiatric in-patients. *Acta Psychiatrica Scandinavica*, *102*, 432–438. ▸ Name up to six authors, then add "et al."
	In-text	(Koremenos, Lipson, & Snidal, 2001) for first reference (Koremenos et al., 2001) for second reference and after.

Journal article online	Reference list	Conway, P. (2003). Truth and reconciliation: The road not taken in Namibia. *Online Journal of Peace and Conflict Resolution*, *5*(1). Retrieved December 26, 2003, from http://www .trinstitute.org/ojpcr/5_1conway.htm Mitchell, T. (2002). McJihad: Islam in the U.S. global order. *Social Text*, *20*(4), 1–18. Retrieved December 28, 2003, from JSTOR database: http://muse.jhu.edu/journals/social_text/ vo20/20.4mitchell.html ▸ Your can omit the URL when citing well-known databases, such as JSTOR or PsycARTICLES.
	In-text	(Conway, 2003) (Mitchell, 2002)

Newspaper or magazine article, no author	Reference list	The United States and the Americas: One history in two halves. (2003, December 13). *Economist*, 36. Strong aftershocks continue in California. (2003, December 26). *New York Times* [national ed.], p. A23. ▸ Newspaper page numbers include p. or pp.
	In-text	("United States and the Americas," 2003) ("Strong aftershocks," 2003)
Newspaper or magazine article with author	Reference list	Bruni, F. (2003, December 26). Pope pleads for end to terrorism and war. *New York Times* [national ed.], p. A21.
	In-text	(Bruni, 2003) or, if necessary, (Bruni, 2003, December 26)
Newspaper or magazine article online	Reference list	Vick, K. (2003, December 27). Quake in Iran kills at least 5,000: Temblor devastates ancient city; officials appeal for assistance. *Washington Post* [online], p. A01. Retrieved January 2, 2004, from http://www.washingtonpost.com/wp-dyn/articles/A31539-2003Dec26.html Jehl, D. (2004, January 1). U.S. hunts terror clues in case of 2 brothers. *New York Times* [online], p. A10. Retrieved February 6, 2004, from ProQuest Newspapers database.
	In-text	(Vick, 2003) or (Vick 2003, December 27)
Review of book	Reference list	Orr, H. A. (2003, August 14). What's not in your genes. [Review of the book *Nature via nurture: Genes, experience, and what makes us human*]. *New York Review of Books, 50*, 38–40.
Unpublished paper, poster session, dissertation, or thesis	Reference list	Tsygankov, A. (2004, February). *Russia's identity and foreign policy choices*. Paper presented at the Program on International Politics, Economics, and Security, University of Chicago.

    ▸ Only the month and year are needed for papers.

Cheng, D. T., Smith, C. N., Thomas, T. L., Richards, J. A., Knight, D. C., Rao, S. M., et al. (2003, June). *Differential reinforcement of stimulus dimensions during human Pavlovian fear conditioning*. Poster session presented at the 9th Annual Meeting of the Organization for Human Brain Mapping, New York, NY.

Reid, P. (1998). *Beginning therapists and difficult clients: An exploratory study*. Unpublished master's thesis, University of Massachusetts, Amherst.

Gomez, C. (2003). *Identifying early indicators for autism in self-regulatory difficulties*. Unpublished doctoral dissertation. Auburn University, Alabama.

In-text	(Tsygankov, 2004)
	(Cheng et al., 2003)
	(Reid, 1998)
	(Gomez, 2003)

Microfilm, microfiche	Reference list	U.S. House of Representatives. Records. Southern Claims Commission. (1871–1880). *First report (1871)*. Washington, DC: National Archives Microfilm Publication, P2257, Frames 0145–0165.

Conservative Party (UK). (1919). *Annual report of the executive committee to central council, March 11–November 18, 1919*. Archives of the British Conservative Party, Microfiche card 143. Woodbridge, CT: Gale/Primary Source Microfilm, 1998. (Original material located in Conservative Party Archive, Bodleian Library, Oxford, UK).

    ▸ You do not need to include the location of the original material, but you are welcome to.

In-text	(U.S. House, 1871–1880)
	(Conservative Party, 1919)

Preprint	Reference list	Williams, A., Leen, T. K., Roberts, P. D. (2003). Random walks for spike-timing dependent plasticity. Preprint. arXiv: q-bio.NC/0312038. Retrieved December 26, 2003, from http://xxx.lanl.gov/PS_cache/q-bio/pdf/0312/0312038.pdf
		▸ arXiv is a collection facility for scientific preprints. The "q-bio" number is its identification number there. ID numbers and URLs are valuable to readers who wish to follow your citation to the database itself.
	In-text	(Williams, Leen, & Roberts, 2003)
Encyclopedia, hard copy and online	Reference list	Balkans: History. (1987). In *Encyclopaedia Britannica* (15th ed., Vol. 14, pp. 570–588). Chicago: Encyclopaedia Britannica. Balkans. *Encyclopaedia Britannica* [online]. Retrieved December 28, 2003, from http://search.eb.com/eb/article?eu=119645 Graham, G. (2002). Behaviorism. In *Stanford encyclopedia of philosophy* [online]. Retrieved January 5, 2004, from http://plato.stanford.edu/entries/behaviorism/
	In-text	("Balkans: History," 1987) ("Balkans," 2003) (Graham, 2002)
Reference book, hard copy and online	Reference list	Pendergast, S., & Pendergast, T. (Eds.). (2003). *Reference guide to world literature* (3rd ed., 2 vols.). Detroit: St. James Press/Thomson-Gale. Pendergast, S., & Pendergast, T. (Eds.). (2003). *Reference guide to world literature*. E-Book. (3rd ed.). Detroit: St. James Press. Colman, A. M. (2001). *A Dictionary of Psychology*. Oxford: Oxford University Press. Retrieved March 16, 2004, from http://www.oxfordreference.com/views/BOOK_SEARCH.html?book=t87 Woods, T. (2003). "The social contract (du

contract social), prose by Jean-Jacques
Rousseau, 1762." In Pendergast, S., &
Pendergast, T. (Eds.), *Reference guide to world
literature* (3rd ed., Vol. 2, pp. 1512–1513).
Detroit: St. James Press/Thomson-Gale.
"Great Britain: Queen's speech opens
Parliament." (2003, November 26).
FirstSearch. Facts On File database. Accession
no. 2003302680.

In-text	(Pendergast & Pendergast, 2003) (Colman, 2001) (Woods, 2003) ("Great Britain: Queen's speech," 2003)

| Dictionary,
hard copy,
online, and
CD-ROM | Reference list | Gerrymander. (2003). *Merriam-Webster's
collegiate dictionary* (11th ed.). Springfield,
MA: Merriam-Webster.
Protest, *v.* (1971). *Compact edition of the Oxford
English dictionary* (Vol. II, p. 2335). Oxford:
Oxford University Press. |

- The word "protest" is both a noun and a verb.
  Here, I am citing the verb.

Class, *n.* (2003). *Dictionary.com*. Retrieved
January 4, 2004, from http://dictionary
.reference.com/search?q=class
Anxious. (2000). *American Heritage Dictionary of
the English Language* (4th ed.). CD-ROM.
Boston: Houghton Mifflin.

In-text	("Protest," 1971)

| Government
document,
hard copy
and online | Reference list | *A bill to promote the national security by
providing for a national defense establishment:
Hearings on S. 758 before the Committee on
Armed Service, Senate.* 80th Cong., 1 (1947). |

- "80th Cong., 1" refers to page one (not to the
  first session). If the reference was to testimony
  by a specific individual, that would appear after
  the date: (1947) (testimony of Gen. George
  Marshall).
- For documents printed by the Government

Government document, hard copy and online (*continued*)		Printing Office, give the full name rather than the initials GPO. U.S. Bureau of the Census. (2000). *Statistical abstracts of the U.S.* Washington, DC: U.S. Bureau of the Census. U.S. Department of Commerce. (2002). *A nation online: How Americans are expanding their use of the Internet.* Retrieved December 30, 2003, from http://www.ntia.doc.gov/ntiahome/dn/anationonline2.pdf Federal Bureau of Investigation. (2001). *Investigation of Charles "Lucky" Luciano.* Part 1A. Retrieved January 2, 2004, from http://foia.fbi.gov/luciano/luciano1a.pdf
	In-text	(*Bill to Promote National Security*, 1947) (U.S. Bureau of the Census, 2000) (U.S. Dept. of Commerce, 2002) (FBI, 2001)
Speech, academic talk, or course lecture	Reference list	Szelenyi, I. (2003, August 17). Presidential address. American Sociological Association. Annual convention. Atlanta, GA. Woodward, A. (2004, April 14). Course lecture. University of Chicago. Chicago, IL.
	In-text	(Szelenyi, 2003) (Woodward, 2004)
Interview	Reference list	Wilson, E. O. (2004, February 1). Personal interview regarding biodiversity. Cambridge, MA.
	In-text	(Wilson, 2004)
Television program	Reference list	Long, T. (Writer), & Moore, S. D. (Director). (2002). Bart vs. Lisa vs. 3rd Grade [Television series episode]. In B. Oakley & J. Weinstein (Producers), *The Simpsons*. Episode: 1403 F55079. Fox.
	In-text	(*Simpsons*, 2002) or ("Bart vs. Lisa," 2002)

Film	Reference list	Huston, J. (Director/Writer). (1941). *Maltese falcon* [Motion picture]. Perf. Humphrey Bogart, Mary Astor, Peter Lorre, Sydney Greenstreet, Elisha Cook Jr. Based on novel by Dashiell Hammett. Warner Studios. United States: Warner Home Video, DVD (2000). ▸ Required: You must include the title, director, studio, and year released. ▸ Optional: the actors, producers, screenwriters, editors, cinematographers, and other information. Include what you need for analysis in your paper, in order of importance to your analysis. Their names appear between the title and the distributor.
	In-text	(*Maltese falcon*, 1941) or (*Maltese falcon*, 2000)
Photograph	Reference list	Adams, Ansel. (1927). *Monolith, the face of Half Dome, Yosemite national park* [photograph]. Art Institute, Chicago.
	In-text	(Adams, 1927)
Software	Reference list	Dreamweaver MX 2004 [Computer software]. (2003). San Francisco: Macromedia. SPSS regression models (12.0 for Windows) [Computer software]. (2003). Chicago: SPSS.
	In-text	(Dreamweaver MX 2004, 2003) (SPSS Regression Models, 2003)
Database	Reference list	Bedford, VA, city of. (2004). *Property tax database.* Retrieved March 15, 2004, from http://www.ci.bedford.va.us/proptax/lookup.shtml *Intellectual Property Treaties, InterAm Database.* (2004). Tucson, AZ: National Law Center for Inter-American Free Trade. Retrieved March 15, 2004, from http://www.natlaw.com/database.htm
	In-text	(Bedford, 2004) (*Intellectual Property Treaties*, 2004)

Diagnostic test	Reference list	Tellegen, A., Ben-Porath, Y. S., McNulty, J. L., Arbisi, P. A., Graham, J. R., & Kaemmer, B. (2001). *MMPI-2 restructured clinical (RC) scales*. Minneapolis: University of Minnesota Press and Pearson Assessments.
		Butcher, J. N., Graham, J. R., Ben-Porath, Y. S., Tellegen, A., Dahlstrom, W. G., & Kaemmer, B. (2001). *Minnesota multiphasic personality inventory-2 (MMPI-2): Manual for administration, scoring and interpretation* (Rev. ed.). Minneapolis: University of Minnesota Press.
		► Manual for administering the test.
		Tellegen, A., Ben-Porath, Y. S., McNulty, J. L., Arbisi, P. A. & Graham, J. R. (2003). *The MMPI-2 restructured clinical (RC) scales: Development, validation, and interpretation*. Minneapolis: University of Minnesota Press and Pearson Assessments.
		► Interpretive manual for the test.
		Microtest Q assessment system software for MMPI-2. (2003). Version 5.07. Minneapolis: Pearson Assessments.
		► Scoring software for the test.
	In-text	(*MMPI-2 RC Scales*, 2001) (*MMPI-2 RC Scales*, 2003) (*Microtest Q*, 2003)
Diagnostic manual	Reference list	American Psychiatric Association. (2000). *Diagnostic and statistical manual of mental disorders* (4th ed. text revision [*DSM-IV-TR*]). Washington, DC: American Psychiatric Association Press.
	In-text	(American Psychiatric Association, *Diagnostic and statistical manual of mental disorders*, 2000) for the first use only. (*DSM-IV-TR*) for second use and later. Title is italicized.

Web site, entire	Reference list	*Digital History* Web site. (2004). S. Mintz (Ed.). Retrieved January 10, 2004, from http://www.digitalhistory.uh.edu/index.cfm?
		Internet Public Library (IPL) (2003, November 17). Retrieved January 5, 2004, from http://www.ipl.org/
		Yale University, History Department home page. (2003). Retrieved January 6, 2004, from http://www.yale.edu/history/
		▸ If a Web site or Web page does not show a date when it was copyrighted or updated, then list (n.d.) where the year normally appears.
	In-text	(Digital History, 2004)
		(Internet Public Library, 2003) or (IPL, 2003)
		(Yale History Department home page, 2003)
Web page	Reference list	Lipson, C. (2004). *Advice on getting a great recommendation.* Retrieved February 1, 2004, from http://www.charleslipson.com/courses/Getting-a-good-recommendation.htm
	In-text	(Lipson, 2004)
Weblog, entries and comments	Reference list	Drezner, D. (2004, February 1). Entry post. Retrieved February 2, 2004, from http://www.danieldrezner.com/blog/
	In-text	(Drezner, 2004)

APA does not permit very many abbreviations in its reference lists. When it does, it sometimes wants them capitalized and sometimes not. Who knows why?

APA: COMMON ABBREVIATIONS IN REFERENCE LIST

chapter	chap.	number	No.	supplement	Suppl.
editor	Ed.	page	p.	translated by	Trans.
edition	ed.	pages	pp.	volume	Vol.
second edition	2nd ed.	part	Pt.	volumes	Vols.
revised edition	Rev. ed.				

CSE CITATIONS FOR THE
BIOLOGICAL SCIENCES

· · · · · · · · · · · · · ·

CSE citations, devised by the Council of Science Editors, are widely used for scientific papers, journals, and books in the life sciences. The citations are based on international principles adopted by the National Library of Medicine.

Actually, the CSE system lets you choose among three ways of citing documents:

- *Citation-sequence:* Citations are numbered (1), (2), (3), in the order they appear in the text. Full references appear at the end of the paper — in the same order.
- *Citation-name:* Citations are numbered, with full references at the end of the paper — in alphabetical order. The first item cited in the text might be number eight on the alphabetical list. It would be cited as (8), wherever it appeared.
- *Name-year:* Citations in the text are given as name and year, such as (McClintock 2004). Full references appear at the end of the paper in alphabetical order, just as they do in APA citations.

Whichever format you choose, use it consistently throughout the paper. Ask your instructor which one she prefers.

Citation-sequence: Cite the first reference in the text as number 1, the second as number 2, and so on. You can use brackets [1], superscripts[1], or parentheses (1). At the end of the paper, list all the items, beginning with the first one cited. The list is *not* alphabetical. If the first item you cite is by Professor Zangwill, then that's the first item in the reference list. If you cite Zangwill's paper again, it's still [1], even if it's the last citation in your paper. If you want to cite several items at once, simply include the number for each one, separated by commas, such as [1,3,9] or [1,3,9] or (1,3,9). If items have successive numbers, use hyphens: 4-6,12-18.

Citation-name: Begin by assembling an alphabetical list of references at the end of the text and numbering them. Each item in the list will have a number, which is used whenever that book or article is cited in the text. If the Zangwill article is thirty-sixth in the alphabetical list, then it is always cited with that number, even if it's the first item you cite in the paper. The next reference in the text might be [23], the one after that might be [12]. Citations can be set as superscripts, in brackets, or in parentheses. If you want to cite several items at once, include a number for each one, such as [4,15,22] or [4,15,22] or (4,15,22). Use hyphens for continuous numbers (1-3). So a citation could be (4,16-18,22).

Name-year: For in-text citations, use the (name-year) format without commas, such as (Cronin and Siegler 2003) and (Siegler and others 2004). The reference list is alphabetical by author and includes all cited articles. If an author has several articles, list the earliest ones first. Follow the same method if an author has published several articles in the same year. List the first one as 2004a, the second as 2004b, and so on by the month of publication. To cite several articles by Susan Lindquist, then, the notation might be (Lindquist 2003d, 2004a, 2004h), referring to those three articles in the reference list.

In the same way, you can also cite articles by different authors within the same reference. Separate them by semicolons, such as (Liebman 2001; Ma and Lindquist 2003; Outeiro and Lindquist 2003).

If the author's name appears in the sentence, you do not need to repeat it in the citation. For example, "According to LaBarbera (2004), this experiment...."

What if LaBarbera had ten or fifteen coauthors? That's certainly possible in the sciences. Articles sometimes have dozens of authors because they include everyone involved in the experiments leading to publication. My colleague Henry Frisch, a high-energy physicist, told me that one of his articles has nearly eight hundred coauthors![1] I grew up in a town with a smaller phone book.

---

1. Professor Frisch's own practice is to list himself as author only if he actually helped write the paper. His practice is unusual, but a number of scientists think he's right and that current practices are unclear and often lax. To correct the problem, some scientists

How many of these authors should you include when you use name-year citations in the text? Don't go overboard. Just list the first seven hundred. If you do that in the first sentence, you'll reach the paper's word limit before you even have to write a second sentence. That's one easy science paper.

Actually, CSE offers clear recommendations. If there are only two authors, list them both, separated by "and." If there are three or more authors, list only the first one, followed by "and others." For example: (LaBarbera and others 2004). Notice, by the way, that CSE uses the English phrase "and others" rather than the Latin "et al.," used in most other citation styles. Later, I'll show you how to handle coauthors in the reference list at the end of the paper.

QUICK COMPARISON OF CSE STYLES		
STYLE	**IN-TEXT CITATIONS**	**REFERENCE LIST AT END OF PAPER**
Citation-sequence	(1), (2), (3), (4)	Items listed in order of their text appearance
Citation-name	(31), (2), (13), (7)	Items listed alphabetically, by author surname
Name-year	(Shapiro 2004)	Items listed alphabetically, by author surname

STYLES OF REFERENCE LISTS

All three styles require reference lists following the text. CSE emphasizes brevity and simplicity for these lists. Instead of using the authors' first names, use only their initials. Omit periods after the initials and don't put spaces between them: Stern HK. Shorten journal names with standard abbreviations, such as those given in the *Index Medicus* system, available online at http://www.nlm.nih.gov/tsd/serials/lji.html.

CSE uses sentence-style capitalization for titles. Capitalize only the first word, proper nouns, and the first word after a colon. Print the titles in normal type rather than italics. Hanging indents are optional.

---

are circulating proposals that would require coauthors to specify how they contributed to joint papers. For Frisch's comments on the metastasizing growth of coauthors, see his Web page, http://hep.uchicago.edu/~frisch.

If you cite something you've read online rather than in print, cite the electronic version. After all, the two versions may differ. To do that, CSE style requires you to add a couple of items to the citation: (1) the date you accessed the document and (2) the fact that it was an Internet document. With CSE style, you need to show when you accessed the article. That comes in brackets after the publication date. You also need to show that you are citing the electronic version. To do that, simply add [Internet] in square brackets, immediately after the journal title.

Print citation	Jacob S, McClintock MK, Zelano B, Ober C. 2002. Paternally inherited HLA alleles are associated with women's choice of male odor. Nat Genet 30:175–9.
Internet citation	Jacob S, McClintock MK, Zelano B, Ober C. 2002 [cited 2004 Feb 2]. Paternally inherited HLA alleles are associated with women's choice of male odor. Nat Genet [Internet]; 30:175–9.

If you wish to include the URL for the article, put it after the page numbers. If there is a document identification number (DOI) or other database number, put it last. There is no period after the DOI.

Internet citation with URL and document ID number	Jacob S, McClintock MK, Zelano B, Ober C. 2002 [cited 2004 Feb 2]. Paternally inherited HLA allelesare associated with women's choice of male odor. Nat Genet [Internet]; 30:175–9. Available from: http://genes.uchicago.edu/fri/ jacob_ober5.pdf. DOI: 10.1038/ng830

This article, like nearly all printed articles, was not modified after it was published. But preprints are often modified and so are articles in electronic journals. You need to include that information in the citation so your readers will know which version you are citing. That information appears in the square brackets, immediately before the date you accessed the item.

Modified paper	Jacob S, McClintock MK, Zelano B, Ober C. 2002 [modified 2004 Jan 20; cited 2004 Feb 2]. Paternally inherited HLA alleles are associated with women's choice of male odor. Nat Genet [Internet]; 30:175–9. Available from: http://

genes.uchicago.edu/fri/jacob_ober5.pdf. DOI:
10.1038/ng830

Don't worry about remembering all these details. There are too many of
them. I'll explain them in the tables that follow and include plenty of examples. If you use this style often, you'll gradually grow familiar with the
fine points.

These tables show CSE recommendations for in-text citations and reference lists, using all three formats. Not every journal follows them exactly,
so you'll see some variation as you read scientific publications. Journals
differ, for example, in how many coauthors they include in the reference list.
Some list only the first three authors before adding "and others." One lists
the first twenty-six. (Imagine being poor coauthor number 27.) The CSE
recommends naming up to ten and then adding "and others."

These tables are based on the forthcoming seventh edition of the CSE
style manual.

CSE: NAME-YEAR SYSTEM		
Journal article	Reference list	Zhang S, Sha Q, Chen HS, Dong J, Jiang R. 2003. Transmission/disequilibrium test based on haplotype sharing for tightly linked markers. Am J Hum Genet 73(3):566–79.
	In-text	(Zhang and others 2003) ▸ If your list includes several publications by Zhang in 2003, your in-text reference should include coauthors to clarify exactly which article you are citing. For example: (Zhang, Sha and others 2003).
Online journal article	Reference list	Bhandari V. 2003 [cited 2004 Jan 2]. The role of nitric oxide in hyperoxia-induced injury to the developing lung. Front Biosci [Internet];8: e361–9. Available from: http://www .bioscience.org/2003/v8/e/1086/list.htm ▸ This journal article is online only. Do *not* add a period at the end of the URL.
	In-text	(Bhandari 2003)

Book, one author	Reference list	Kardong KV. 2002. Vertebrates: Comparative anatomy, function, evolution. New York: McGraw-Hill.
		▸ If the publisher's city is well known, you may omit the state.
	In-text	(Kardong 2002)
		▸ To cite the same author for works written in several years:
		(Kardong 1996, 2000, 2002a, 2002b)
		▸ To cite works by authors with the same surname published in the same year, include the authors' initials:
		(Kardong KV 2002; Kardong LS 2002)
Book, multiple authors	Reference list	Kohane IS, Kho AT, Butte AJ. 2003. Microarrays for an integrative genomics. Cambridge (MA): MIT Press.
		▸ In the reference list, name up to ten authors, then add "and others."
	In-text	(Kohane and others 2003)
		▸ If there are just two authors, name them both:
		(Kohane and Kho 1995)
Book, multiple editions	Reference list	Snell RS. 2004. Clinical anatomy. 7th ed. Philadelphia: Lippincott Williams & Wilkins.
		▸ For a revised edition, the phrase "Rev. ed." appears where "7th ed." currently does.
	In-text	(Snell 2004)
Book, multiple editions, no author	Reference list	Publication manual of the American Psychological Association. 2001. 5th ed. Washington (DC): American Psychological Association.
	In-text	(Publication manual . . . 2001)
		▸ Do not use "Anonymous" in place of the author name. Instead, use the first word or first few words of the title and an ellipsis, followed by the date.

Book, edited	Reference list	Marr JJ, Nilsen TW, Komuniecki RW, editors. 2003. Molecular medical parasitology. Amsterdam (Netherlands): Academic Press.
	In-text	(Marr and others 2003)
Chapter in book	Reference list	Kramer JA. 2003. Overview of the tools for microarray analysis: Transcription profiling, DNA chips, and differential display. In: Krawetz SA, Womble DD, editors. Introduction to bioinformatics: A theoretical and practical approach. Totowa (NJ): Humana Press. Pp. 637–63.
	In-text	(Kramer 2003)
Government document	Reference list	[NHLBI] National Heart, Lung, and Blood Institute (US), National High Blood Pressure Education Program. 2003 [cited 2003 Oct 12]. The seventh report of the Joint National Committee on Prevention, Detection, Evaluation, and Treatment of High Blood Pressure (JNC7) [Internet]. Bethesda (MD): National Heart, Lung, and Blood Institute (US). Available from: http://www.nhlbi.nih.gov/ guidelines/hypertension/ index.htm ▸ If an organization is both author and publisher, the name may be abbreviated as publisher. For example, Bethesda (MD): The Institute.
	In-text	(NHLBI 2003)
Database	Reference list	[PDB] Protein Data Bank. 2004 [cited 2004 Jan 5]. Available from: http://www.rcsb.org/pdb/
	In-text	(Protein Data Bank 2004) or (PDB 2004)
Other Internet documents	Reference list	[CSE] Council of Science Editors. 2003 [cited 2003 Oct 12]. Citing the Internet: Formats for bibliographic citation [Internet]. Reston (VA): Council of Science Editors. Available from:

> http://www.councilscienceeditors.org/
> publications/citing_internet.cfm
>
> ▸ Where this citation says only [Internet], yours
>   might say [monograph on Internet] or
>   [database on Internet].

In-text   (CSE 2003)

The next table shows CSE references using citation-sequence and citation-name formats. The main difference from the previous table is that the date appears later in the reference. The list does not use hanging indents. I have used the same articles, in case you want to compare formats.

CSE: CITATION-SEQUENCE AND CITATION-NAME SYSTEMS		
Journal article	Reference list	Zhang S, Sha Q, Chen HS, Dong J, Jiang R. Transmission/disequilibrium test based on haplotype sharing for tightly linked markers. Am J Hum Genet 2003;73(3):566–79.
Online journal article	Reference list	Bhandari V. The role of nitric oxide in hyperoxia-induced injury to the developing lung. Front Biosci [Internet] 2003 [cited 2004 Jan 2];8:e361–9. Available from: http://www.bioscience.org/2003/v8/e/1086/list.htm ▸ This journal article is online only.
Book, one author	Reference list	Kardong KV. Vertebrates: Comparative anatomy, function, evolution. New York: McGraw-Hill; 2002. ▸ If the publisher's city is well known, you may omit the state abbreviation, if you wish.
Book, multiple authors	Reference list	Kohane IS, Kho AT, Butte AJ. Microarrays for an integrative genomics. Cambridge (MA): MIT Press; 2003. ▸ In the reference list, name up to ten authors, then add "and others."

Book, multiple editions	Reference list	Snell RS. Clinical anatomy. 7th ed. Philadelphia: Lippincott Williams & Wilkins; 2004. ▸ For a revised edition, use "Rev. ed." in place of "7th ed."
Book, multiple editions, no author	Reference list	Publication manual of the American Psychological Association. 5th ed. Washington (DC): American Psychological Association; 2001.
Book, edited	Reference list	Marr JJ, Nilsen TW, Komuniecki RW, editors. Molecular medical parasitology. Amsterdam (Netherlands): Academic Press; 2003.
Chapter in book	Reference list	Kramer JA. Overview of the tools for microarray analysis: Transcription profiling, DNA chips, and differential display. In: Krawetz SA, Womble DD, editors. Introduction to bioinformatics: A theoretical and practical approach. Totowa (NJ): Humana Press; 2003. Pp. 637–63.
Government document	Reference list	National Heart, Lung, and Blood Institute (US), National High Blood Pressure Education Program. The seventh report of the Joint National Committee on Prevention, Detection, Evaluation, and Treatment of High Blood Pressure (JNC7) [Internet]. Bethesda (MD): National Heart, Lung, and Blood Institute (US); 2003 [cited 2003 Oct 12]. Available from: http://www.nhlbi.nih.gov/guidelines/hypertension/index.htm
Database	Reference list	Protein Data Bank (PDB). 2004 [cited 2004 Jan 5]. Available from: http://www.rcsb.org/pdb/
Other Internet documents	Reference list	Council of Science Editors. Citing the Internet: Formats for bibliographic citation [Internet]. Reston (VA): Council of Science Editors; 2003 [cited 2003 Oct 12]. Available http://www.councilscienceeditors.org/publications/citing_internet.cfm

National Library of Medicine. Recommended
formats for bibliographic citation, supplement:
Internet formats [Internet]. 2001 [cited 2004 Jan
5]. Available from: http://www.nlm.nih.gov/
pubs/formats/internet.pdf

► Where this citation says [Internet], yours might
say [monograph on Internet] or [database on
Internet].

Although individual references (shown above) are the same for both the
citation-sequence and citation-name systems, their full reference lists are
compiled in different orders.

Order of items within reference lists:

• Citation-name system: alphabetical by author.
• Citation-sequence system: order of first appearance in the text.

To illustrate, let's take the opening sentence of an article and show how
each style would handle the citations and reference list.

CSE: CITATION-SEQUENCE SYSTEM (ILLUSTRATION OF REFERENCE LIST ORDER)

Opening sentence   This research deals with the ABC transporter family and
builds on prior studies by Zeleznikar and others,[1] Randak
and Welsh,[2] and Dean and others.[3]

Reference list   [1] Zeleznikar RJ, Dzeja PP, Goldberg, ND. Adenylate
(in order of   kinase-catalyzed phosphoryl transfer couples ATP
appearance in text) utilization with its generation by glycolysis in intact
muscle. J Biol Chem 1995;270(13):7311–9. PMID:
7706272

[2] Randak C, Welsh MJ. An intrinsic adenylate kinase
activity regulates gating of the ABC transporter CFTR.
Cell [Internet]. 2003 [cited 2003 Oct 12];115(7):837–50.
PMID: 14697202

[3] Dean M, Rzhetsky A, Allikmets R. The human ATP-
binding cassette (ABC) transporter superfamily.
Genome Res [Internet]. 2001 [cited 2001 Apr
3];11(7):1156–66. PMID: 11435397

► Zeleznikar's article is listed first because it is the first one
mentioned in the text.

CSE: CITATION-NAME SYSTEM (ILLUSTRATION OF REFERENCE LIST ORDER)

Opening sentence	This research deals with the ABC transporter family and builds on prior studies by Zeleznikar and others,[3] Randak and Welsh,[2] and Dean and others.[1]
Reference list (alphabetical)	[1] Dean M, Rzhetsky A, Allikmets R. The human ATP-binding cassette (ABC) transporter superfamily. Genome Res [Internet]. 2001 [cited 2001 Apr 3];11(7): 1156–66. PMID: 11435397
	[2] Randak C, Welsh MJ. An intrinsic adenylate kinase activity regulates gating of the ABC transporter CFTR. Cell [Internet]. 2003 [cited 2003 Oct 12];115(7):837–50. PMID: 14697202
	[3] Zeleznikar RJ, Dzeja PP, Goldberg ND. Adenylate kinase-catalyzed phosphoryl transfer couples ATP utilization with its generation by glycolysis in intact muscle. J Biol Chem 1995;270(13):7311–9. PMID: 7706272
	▸ Zeleznikar's article is listed last because it is last alphabetically.

The two systems, citation-sequence and citation-name, present *each item* in the reference list the same way. What's different are (1) the *order* of items in the reference list and (2) their *citation numbers* in the text.

There's one more item you may wish to include in your citations: the PMID number. All medical articles have this electronic tag, which identifies them within the comprehensive PubMed database. The PMID appears as the last item in the citation and is *not* followed by a period:

Dean M, Rzhetsky A, Allikmets R. The human ATP-binding cassette (ABC) transporter superfamily. Genome Res [Internet]. 2001 [cited 2001 Apr 3]; 11(7):1156–66. PMID: 11435397

The PubMed database, covering more than four thousand biomedical journals, was developed at the National Library of Medicine and it is available online at www.ncbi.nlm.nih.gov/entrez.

Detailed information about CBE citations for the sciences can be found in

- *Scientific Style and Format: The CBE Manual for Authors, Editors, and Publishers*, 6th ed. (Cambridge: Cambridge University Press; 1994). Published for the Council of Biology Editors, now renamed the Council of Science Editors.

The sixth edition covers citations in two styles: name-date and citation-sequence. The seventh edition, due out in 2004–2005, adds citation-name. This chapter conforms to the forthcoming edition, thanks to the generous assistance of two scholars working on the new volume: Peggy Robinson (chair of the CSE's Style Manual Subcommittee) and Karen J. Patrias (of the National Library of Medicine, Reference Section).

AMA CITATIONS FOR THE BIOMEDICAL SCIENCES, MEDICINE, AND NURSING

9

• • • • • • • • • • • • • •

AMA citations are used in biomedical research, medicine, nursing, and some related fields of biology. They are based on the *American Medical Association Manual of Style: A Guide for Authors and Editors*, 9th ed. (Baltimore, MD: Williams & Wilkins, 1998).

Citations are numbered (1), (2), (3), in the order they appear in the text. Full references appear at the end of the paper — in the same order. For coauthored books and articles, you should list up to six authors. If there are more, list only the first three, followed by "et al." Rather than using the authors' first names, use their initials (without periods) and do not put spaces between the initials: Lipson CH. Abbreviate the title of journals. There's a standard list of abbreviations (the *Index Medicus* system) available online at http://www.nlm.nih.gov/tsd/serials/lji.html.

	AMA CITATIONS
Journal article	Cooper DS. Hyperthyroidism. *Lancet.* 2003;362:459–468. Cummings JL, Cole G. Alzheimer disease. *JAMA.* 2002;287:2335–2338. Beinart SC, Sales AE, Spertus JA, Plomondon ME, Every NR, Rumsfeld JS. Impact of angina burden and other factors on treatment satisfaction after acute coronary syndromes. *Am Heart J.* 2003;146:646–652. ► Name up to six authors in articles or books. If there are more, name the first three, then use "et al." This article, for example, has thirteen listed authors: Wen G, Mahata SK, Cadman P, et al. Both rare and common polymorphisms contribute functional variation at

CHGA, a regulator of catecholamine physiology. *Am J Hum Genet.* 2004;74:197–207.

> ► Journal titles are abbreviated without periods. (There is a period after "*Genet.*" only because it is the last word in the journal's title.) Likewise, there is a period after "et al" only because a period always follows the final author's name.

Online journal article

Bhandari V. The role of nitric oxide in hyperoxia-induced injury to the developing lung. *Front Biosci* [serial online]. 2003;8:e361–e369. Available from: http://www.bioscience.org/2003/v8/e/1086/list.htm. Accessed October 12, 2003.

> ► This journal article is online only.

Book, one author

Krimsky S. *Science in the Private Interest: Has the Lure of Profits Corrupted Biomedical Research?* Lanham, Md: Rowman & Littlefield; 2003.

> ► Notice how the state name is abbreviated.

Beasley RW. *Beasley's Surgery of the Hand.* New York, NY: Thieme; 2003.

Book, multiple authors

Marso SP, Stern DM. *Diabetes and Cardiovascular Disease: Integrating Science and Clinical Medicine.* Philadelphia, Pa: Lippincott Williams & Wilkins; 2003.

Book, multiple editions

Snell RS. *Clinical Anatomy.* 7th ed. Philadelphia, Pa: Lippincott Williams & Wilkins; 2004.

Brown MA, Semelka RC. *MRI: Basic Principles and Applications.* 3rd ed. Hoboken, NJ: Wiley-Liss; 2003.

> ► The edition number appears between the book's title and the place of publication.
> ► For a revised edition, use "Rev. ed." in place of the specific edition.

Book, multiple editions, no author

Dorland's Illustrated Medical Dictionary. 30th ed. Philadelphia, Pa: Saunders; 2003.

Nursing 2004 Drug Handbook. 24th ed. Springhouse, Pa: Springhouse; 2003.

Other reference books	Juo P-S. *Concise Dictionary of Biomedicine and Molecular Biology.* 2nd ed. Boca Raton, Fla: CRC Press; 2001. Dox IG, Melloni BJ. *Melloni's Illustrated Medical Dictionary.* 4th ed. London, England: Parthenon Publishing; 2002. Fuster V, Alexander RW, O'Rourke RA, eds. *Hurst's The Heart.* Vol 2. 10th ed. New York, NY: McGraw Hill; 2002. ▸ "Vol" does not have a period. AMA eliminates periods after abbreviations.
Book, edited	Marr JJ, Nilsen TW, Komuniecki RW, eds. *Molecular Medical Parasitology.* Amsterdam, Neth: Academic Press; 2003.
Chapter in edited book	Kramer JA. Overview of the tools for microarray analysis: Transcription profiling, DNA chips, and differential display. In: Krawetz SA, Womble DD, eds. *Introduction to Bioinformatics: A Theoretical and Practical Approach.* Totowa, NJ: Humana Press; 2003:637–663.
Unpublished material or preprint	Shankar RP, Partha P, Shenoy NK, and Brahmadathan KN. Investigation of antimicrobial use pattern in the intensive treatment unit of a teaching hospital in western Nepal. Preprint. July 26, 2002. Clinmed/2002050008. Available at: http://clinmed.netprints.org/cgi/content/full/ 2002050008v1. Accessed March 7, 2004.
Published letter or comment	Hecht H, Rumberger JA, Budoff MJ. C-reactive protein and electron beam tomography [letter]. *Circulation.* 2003;107: e123–e124.
Personal comment, untitled lecture, or informal communication	Mass DP. Lecture on hand surgery. February 2, 2004. ▸ Using AMA style, your reference list may include lectures and public talks, but not personal communications such as letters and private discussions.
DVD or CD	Amiel S, Mukharjee A, Aitken V. *Essential of Endocrinology III: Diabetes* [CD-ROM]. London, England: Royal Society of Medicine Press; 2002. National Library of Medicine. *Changing the Face of Medicine* [interviews on DVD]. Washington, DC: Friends of the National Library of Medicine; 2004.

Database	Protein Data Bank [database online]. Available at: http://www.rcsb.org/pdb/. Accessed January 28, 2004. National Center for Health Statistics. NHIS 2002 data release. Available at: ftp://ftp.cdc.gov/pub/Health_Statistics/NCHS/Datasets/NHIS/2002/. Accessed January 28, 2004.
Government document	Agency for Healthcare Research and Quality. *Ephedra and Ephedrine for Weight Loss and Athletic Performance Enhancement: Clinical Efficacy and Side Effects.* Washington, DC: US Dept of Health and Human Services; 2001. National Heart, Lung, and Blood Institute (US), National High Blood Pressure Education Program. *The Seventh Report of the Joint National Committee on Prevention, Detection, Evaluation, and Treatment of High Blood Pressure* (JNC7) [Internet]. Bethesda, Md: National Heart, Lung, and Blood Institute (US); 2003. Available at: http://www.nhlbi.nih.gov/guidelines/hypertension/index.htm. Accessed November 12, 2003.
Other Internet documents	US Preventive Services Task Force, Agency for Healthcare Research and Quality Web site. Screening for Prostate Cancer: Recommendations and Rationale. Available at: http://www.ahrq.gov/clinic/3rduspstf/prostatescr/prostaterr.htm. Accessed January 28, 2004.

To illustrate how these citations appear in the text, let's take the opening sentence of an article.

AMA (ILLUSTRATION OF REFERENCE LIST ORDER)

Opening sentence	This research deals with the ABC transporter family and builds on prior studies by Zeleznikar et al,[1] Randak and Welsh,[2] and Dean et al.[3]
Reference list (in order of appearance in text)	[1] Zeleznikar RJ, Dzeja PP, Goldberg, ND. Adenylate kinase-catalyzed phosphoryl transfer couples ATP utilization with its generation by glycolysis in intact muscle. *J Biol Chem.* 1995;270(13):7311–7319.

Reference list
(in order of
appearance in text)
(continued)

[2] Randak C, Welsh MJ. An intrinsic adenylate kinase
    activity regulates gating of the ABC transporter CFTR.
    Cell [Internet]. 2003;115(7):837–850.
[3] Dean M, Rzhetsky A, Allikmets, R. The human ATP-
    binding cassette (ABC) transporter superfamily.
    Genome Res [Internet]. 2001;11(7):1156–1166.

► Zeleznikar's article is listed first because it is the first one
  mentioned in the text. Notice that "et al" does not include
  a period when it is used in sentences, according to AMA
  style.

Finally, all medical articles have an electronic identification number,
known as a PMID. You are not required to include it, but it often helps your
readers and will help you, too, if you need to return to the article. The PMID
appears as the last item in the citation and is followed by a period:

Randak C, Welsh MJ. An intrinsic adenylate kinase activity regulates gating of the ABC transporter CFTR. *Cell* [Internet]. 2003;115(7):837–850.
PMID: 14697202.

The PMID identifies the document within the PubMed database, which
includes virtually all biomedical journals. This database was developed at
the National Library of Medicine and it is available online at www.ncbi.nlm
.nih.gov/entrez.

ACS CITATIONS FOR CHEMISTRY

. . . .

ACS CITATIONS IN CHEMISTRY

The American Chemical Society has its own style guide, which gives you a choice of citation formats:

- In-text citations with name and year, similar to APA or CSE. The reference list is alphabetized and appears at the end of the paper.
- Numbered citations, with a reference list at the end of the paper. End references are numbered in the order they appear in the text. These numbered citations, as they appear in the text itself, are either
  - superscript, such as[23], or
  - parenthesis with the number in italics, such as (*23*).

Each format is used by scores of chemistry journals, and your instructor may prefer one over the other. Whichever one you choose, use it consistently throughout the paper.

Fortunately, you collect the same information for either format. In fact, the items in the reference list are presented exactly the same way, whether the list is numbered or alphabetized.

- The author's last name appears first, followed by a comma and then initials (instead of given names), such as Fenn, J. B. Initials are followed by periods.
- Instead of "page," the reference list uses "p" and "pp" without periods.
- For books
  - Include the title and italicize it. That's true for edited books, too.

- Put the publisher's name before the location, as in CRC Press: Boca Raton, FL.
- Include the year of publication, using normal typeface, such as Wiley-Interscience: New York; 2004.
- Show pagination in books by using "pp" — for example: CRC Press: Boca Raton, FL, 2004; pp 507–15.
- For edited books, you may include (or omit) the titles of specific chapters; just be consistent.
- For journals
  - Include the journal title, abbreviated and italicized, such as *J. Am. Chem. Soc.*
  - Include the year of publication in **boldface,** the volume number in italics, and the first page number (or total pages) of the article in normal type, such as *Org. Lett.* **2004**, *3*, 215.
  - Show pagination in articles *without* using "pp" — for example: *Chem. Eng. News.* **2004**, *82*, 39–40.
  - Omit titles of journal articles.

There is no explanation for these mysterious details. My guess: the chemists were overcome by fumes many years ago, and the odd results are now beloved traditions.

ACS (CHEMISTRY): IN-TEXT CITATIONS AND REFERENCE LIST		
Journal article	Reference list	Zhao, S.; Liao, X.; Cook, J. M. *Org. Lett.* **2002**, *4*, 687. ▸ Article title is always omitted. ▸ Year of publication is in boldface; volume number is italicized. ▸ Journal titles are italicized and abbreviated according to the Chemical Abstracts Service Source Index (CASSI).
	In-text	(Zhao et al., 2002)
Online journal article	Reference list	Wilson, E. *Chem. Eng. News* [Online]. **2003**, *81*, 35–36.
	In-text	(Wilson, 2003)

Book, one author	Reference list	Eberhardt, M. K. *Reactive Oxygen Metabolites: Chemistry and Medical Consequences*. CRC Press: Boca Raton, FL, 2001; pp 23–42. ▸ Or: Chapter 3 instead of the pagination.
	In-text	(Eberhardt, 2001)
Book, multiple authors	Reference list	Buncel, E.; Dust, J. M. *Carbanion Chemistry: Structures and Mechanisms*. American Chemical Society: Washington, DC, 2003. ▸ What if there are many authors? The *ACS Style Guide* says to name them all. It also notes that some chemistry journals list only the first ten, followed by a semicolon and "et al."
	In-text	(Buncel and Dust, 2003) ▸ Include up to two names for in-text citations. If there are three or more, use this form: (Buncel et al., 2003)
Book, multiple editions	Reference list	Sorenson, W. R.; Sweeny, W.; Campbell, T. W. *Preparative Methods of Polymer Chemistry*, 3rd ed.; Wiley-Interscience: New York, 2001. ▸ For a revised edition, use "Rev. ed." instead of "3rd ed."
	In-text	(Sorenson et al., 2001)
Book, multiple volumes	Reference list	Shore, B. W. *The Theory of Coherent Atomic Excitation: Multilevel Atoms and Incoherence*. Wiley: New York, 1990; Vol. 2.
	In-text	(Shore, vol. 2, 1990)
Book, multiple editions, no author	Reference list	*McGraw-Hill Encyclopedia of Science and Technology*, 9th ed.; McGraw-Hill: New York, 2002; 20 vols.
	In-text	(McGraw-Hill, 2002) ▸ To cite a particular volume: (McGraw-Hill, vol. 6, 2002)

| Book, edited | Reference list | *Oxidative Delignification Chemistry: Fundamentals and Catalysis*; Argyropoulos, D. S., Ed.; American Chemical Society: Washington, DC, 2001. |
| | In-text | (Argyropoulos, 2001) |

Chapter in edited book	Reference list	Wilson, S. R., et al. In *Fullerenes: Chemistry, Physics, and Technology*; Kadish, K. M., Ruoff, R. S., Eds.; Wiley-Interscience: New York, 2000; pp 91–176.
		▸ Or
		Wilson, S. R.; Schuster, D. I.; Nuber, B.; Meier, M. S.; Maggini, M.; Prato, M.; Taylor, R. In *Fullerenes: Chemistry, Physics, and Technology*; Kadish, K. M., Ruoff, R. S., Eds.; Wiley-Interscience: New York, 2000; pp 91–176.
		▸ You may include or omit the chapter title; just be consistent.
		▸ How many authors should you list? If there are only two, list both (Jones and Smith). If there are more, the *ACS Style Guide* says to list them as (Jones et al.). In practice, many chemical journals list up to nine or ten authors; for larger numbers, they list only the first author plus "et al."
	In-text	(Wilson et al., 2000)
		▸ Normally use only one or two names for in-text citations. Occasionally, though, you will find top chemistry journals citing more authors, such as: (Wilson, Schuster, Nuber, Meier, Maggini, Prato, and Taylor, 2000)

| Chemical abstracts | Reference list | Taneda, A.; Shimizu, T.; Kawazoe, Y. *J. Phys.: Condens. Matter* **2001**, *13(16)*, L305–312 (Eng.); *Chem. Abstr.* **2001**, *134*, 372018a. |
| | | ▸ This article by Taneda was published in a journal and referenced in *Chemical Abstracts*. This citation shows a reference to both the full article and the abstract. The abstract always comes |

second, separated from the article by a
semicolon.

Taneda, A.; Shimizu, T.; Kawazoe, Y. *Chem. Abstr.*
2001, *134*, 372018a.

▸ Same article, but shown only as mentioned in
Chemical Abstracts. It is better to refer to the full
published article than the abstract, but that
requires you actually examine the full article.

Chem. Abstr. **2001**, *134*, 372018a.

▸ This is the same article, referred to solely by its
Chemical Abstract number. That number —
134, 372018a — is the CAS accession number.
The number *134* is the volume and 372018a is
the abstract number in the print version of
Chemical Abstracts.

▸ In some earlier editions of *Chemical Abstracts,*
there are several abstracts per page. Abstract f on
page 1167 can be cited as 1167f (or 1167f).

▸ It is usually better to include the authors, as in
the previous references to Taneda et al.

	In-text	(Taneda et al., 2001) (*Chem. Abstr.*, 2001)
Conference paper	Reference list	Haskard, C. A.; Schaupt, I.; Weller, M. G. Presented at the Xth International Conference on Harmful Algae, St. Pete Beach, FL, October 2002; Poster.
	In-text	(Haskard, Schaupt, Weller, 2002)
Government document	Reference list	Substance Abuse and Mental Health Services Administration. *Keeping Youth Drug Free.* DHHS Publication No. (SMA) 3772; Center for Substance Abuse Prevention: Rockville, MD, 2003. Supplemental Environmental Impact Statement for the Airborne Laser Program. *Fed. Regist.* **2003**, *68* (163), 50756–50760. ▸ The *Federal Register* is treated like a journal.
	In-text	(*Keeping Youth Drug Free*, 2003)

Patent	Reference list	Searle, R. G. Carbon Dioxide Recovery in an Ethylene to Ethylene Oxide Production Process. U.S. Patent 6495609, 2002. ▸ It is also acceptable to omit the name of the patent.
	In-text	(Searle, 2002)
CD or DVD	Reference list	Luceigh, B. A. *Chem TV: Organic Chemistry* 3.0 [CD-ROM], 2004.
	In-text	(Luceigh, 2004)
Internet	Reference list	Biochemical Periodic Tables. http://umbbd.ahc .umn.edu/periodic/links.html (accessed Jan 2004). ▸ If the page has an author, his name and initial appear before the title of the page: Oxtoby, J. Biochemical Periodic Tables. http:// . . . .
	In-text	(Oxtoby, 2004)

Detailed information on ACS citations is available in

• Janet S. Dodd, ed., *The ACS Style Guide: A Manual for Authors and Editors*, 2nd ed. (Washington, DC: American Chemical Society, 1997).

11

PHYSICS, ASTROPHYSICS, AND ASTRONOMY CITATIONS

. . . .

AIP CITATIONS IN PHYSICS

Physics citations are based on the *AIP Style Manual*, 4th ed. (New York: American Institute of Physics, 1990). Most physics journals use numbered citations in the text. Items appear in the numbered reference list in the order they appear in the text. The items are not indented. (A few physics journals use the author-year style instead. It has an alphabetized reference list with hanging indents.)

Whichever format is used, individual items in the reference list look the same, at least for articles and preprints (which are the way researchers communicate). References are brief: Authors' names (M. Shochet and S. Nagel), abbreviated journal title, **boldface number for the journal issue**, first page number of the article, and, finally, the year in parentheses.

AIP (PHYSICS): REFERENCE LIST

Journal articles	[1] D. Groom et al., Euro. Phys. J. C **15**, 1 (2000).
	[2] J. Wisdom, Nucl. Phys. B **2** (Proc. Suppl.), 391 (1987).
	► The article's title is always omitted. Journal titles are abbreviated.
	► The publication volume (or issue number) and series are in boldface. For example, if a reference is to an article in *Physical Letters B*, issue number 466, page 415, then it appears as Phys. Lett. B **466**, 415 (1999).
Online journal article	[#] Y. Nakayama and S. Akita, New J. Phys. **5**, 128 (2003). <http://ej.iop.org/links/57/Hd+yfNDozFMnm2H8QoyUKA/njp3_1_128.pdf>.

Online journal article (*continued*)	▸ This is an online-only journal. ▸ The citation may also include a DOI or PII after the URL. DOI is a digital object identifier. PII is a publisher item identifier. Both are ways of uniquely identifying electronic documents. For the Nakayama and Akita article, DOI: 10.1088/1367-2630/5/1/128; PII: S1367-2630(03)65453-4. ▸ Online articles are referenced the same way as articles in print, except that they may include an electronic article number (if one is available), instead of this issue and page number. Example: Phys. Rev. B **63**, 012013 (2001).
Preprint	[#] F. Zantow, O. Kaczmarek, F. Karsch, P. Petreczky, preprint, hep-lat/0301015 (2003). ⟨http://www.thphys .uni-heidelberg.de/hep-lat/0301.html⟩. [#] A. J. M. Medved, preprint, hep-th/0301010J (2003). ⟨http://arxiv.org/abs/hep-th/0301010⟩. Published in High Energy Phys. **5**, 008 (2003). ⟨http://www.iop.org/ EJ/abstract/1126-6708/2003/05/008/⟩. ▸ hep-th = Heidelberg High Energy Physics Preprint Service, e-prints on theoretical physics; hep-lat = e-prints on lattices.
Book, one author	[#] P. Phillips, *Advanced Solid State Physics* (Westview, Boulder, CO, 2003).
Book, multiple authors	[#] J. E. Marsden and T. S. Ratiu, *Introduction to Mechanics and Symmetry* (Springer, New York, 1994). ▸ The *AIP Style Manual* does not say how many authors you should list. If the list is long, however, name only the first and add "et al." Example: Marsden et al., *Introduction* . . . .
Book, multiple editions	[#] G. Börner, *The Early Universe*, 4th ed. (Springer, Berlin, 2003).
Book, multiple volumes	[#] H. S. W. Massey, E. H. S. Burhop, and H. B. Gilbody, editors, *Electronic and Ionic Phenomena*, 5 vols. (Clarendon Press, Oxford, 1969–74).
Book, edited	[#] P. Boffi, D. Piccinin, M. C. Ubaldi, editors, *Infrared Holography for Optical Communications: Techniques,*

Materials, and Devices (Springer-Verlag, New York, 2003).

Chapter in edited book	[#] W. Riddle and H. Lee, in *Biomedical Uses of Radiation*, edited by W. R. Hendee (Wiley-VCH, Weinheim, Germany, 1999).
Database	[#] National Institutes of Standards and Technology, Physics Laboratory, Physical Reference Base. ‹http://physics.nist.gov/PhysRefData/contents.html›.

CITATIONS IN ASTROPHYSICS AND ASTRONOMY

Astronomy and astrophysics don't use AIP/physics citation style or, for that matter, any single format. But most leading journals are fairly similar. They generally use (author-year) citations in the text, followed by an alphabetical reference list. The reference list follows some fairly common rules. It generally

- uses hanging indents;
- contains no bold or italics;
- uses authors' initials rather than their first names;
- joins coauthors' names with an ampersand "&";
- puts the publication date immediately after the authors' name (with no comma between the name and date);
- omits the titles of articles;
- includes titles for books and gives publisher information;
- abbreviates journal names, often reducing them to a couple of initials;
- lists only the first page of an article; and
- ends references without a period.

Because there's no published style manual for astronomy and astrophysics, citation formats vary. I've standardized them, based on the most common forms in the leading journals. Here are some illustrations, based on *Astronomy and Astrophysics* and the *Astrophysical Journal*, with a little tweaking for consistency.

ASTRONOMY AND ASTROPHYSICS: REFERENCE LISTS

Journal articles	Boldyrev, S. 2002, ApJ, 569, 841
	Collin, S., Boisson, C., Mouchet, M., et al. 2002, A&A, 388, 771
	Ferrarese, L., & Merritt, D. 2001, ApJ, 555, L79

Journal articles, several by same authors	Fürst, E., Reich, W., Reich, P., & Reif, K. 1990a, A&AS, 85, 691
	Fürst, E., Reich, W., Reich, P., & Reif, K. 1990b, A&AS, 85, 805
	Kennicutt, R. 1982a, AJ, 87, 255
	Kennicutt, R. 1982b, ApJ, 253, 101
	Yu, Q. 2002, MNRAS, 331, 935
	Yu, Q., & Tremaine, S. 2002, MNRAS, 335, 965

▸ Fürst et al. are listed as 1990a and 1990b because they have the same coauthors.

▸ Kennicut's 1982 articles are listed as 1982a and 1982b because they have the same author.

▸ Yu's articles are both listed as 2002 (without "a" and "b") because they do not have identical authorship.

Online article	Russeil, D. 2003, A&A 397, 133 DOI: 10.1051/0004-6361: 20021504

▸ *All* astronomy, astrophysics, and physics articles are online and available through standard scientific databases. Adding the document identifier or other search information may help your readers find them more easily.

Preprint	Barth, A. J., Ho, L. C., & Sargent, W. L. W. 2002, ApJ, to appear [astro-ph/0209562]
	Cordes, J. M., & Lazio, T. J. 2002, preprint [astro-ph/0207156]
	Ergma, E., & Sarna, M. J. 2002, A&A, submitted [astro-ph/0203433]

Book, one author	De Young, D. S. 2002, The Physics of Extragalactic Radio Sources (Chicago: University of Chicago Press)
	Krolik, J. H. 1999, Active Galactic Nuclei (Princeton: Princeton University Press)

Book, multiple authors	Schrijver, C. J., & Zwaan, C. 2000, Solar and Stellar Magnetic Activity (Cambridge: Cambridge University Press)
Book in a series	Slane, P. O., & Gaensler, B. M., eds., 2002, Neutron Stars in Supernova Remnants (San Francisco: ASP), ASP Conf. Ser. 271
Chapter in edited book	Johnson, H. L. 1968, in Nebulae and Interstellar Matter, ed. B. M. Middlehurst & L. M. Aller (Chicago: University of Chicago Press), 5
Chapter in a book in a series	Arnaud, K. A. 1996, in Astronomical Data Analysis Software Systems V, ed. G. Jacoby & J. Barnes (San Francisco: ASP), ASP Conf. Ser. 101, 17 Lacey, C. K. 2002, in Neutron Stars in Supernova Remnants, ed. Patrick O. Slane & Bryan M. Gaensler (San Francisco: ASP), ASP Conf. Ser. 271, 383 Rieger, F. M., & Mannheim, K. 2001, in High Energy Gamma-Ray Astronomy, ed. F. A. Aharonian & H. Völk (Melville, NY: AIP), AIP Conf. Proc. 558, 716
Unpublished	Egan, M. P., Price, S. D., Moshir, M. M., et al. 1999, Air Force Research Lab. Tech. Rep. no. AFRL-VS. T. R. 1999-1522 Fiore, F., Guainazzi, M., & Grandi, P. 1999, Cookbook for BeppoSAX NFI Spectral Analysis, available by ftp from legacy.gsfc.nasa.gov/sax/doc/software_docs/saxabc_v1.2.ps Kranich, D. 2001, Ph.D. Diss., Technische Universität München
Internet	Skyview, the Internet Virtual Telescope ‹http://skyview.gsfc.nasa.gov›

Researchers in the physical sciences often cite unpublished research, usually conference papers or work-in-progress that will be published later. Known as preprints (or e-prints), these papers are at the cutting edge of the field and are collected in electronic document archives. Besides collections

at major research institutions, there's a huge collection at arXiv.org (http://
www.arxiv.org), with mirror sites around the world. Papers are readily accessible and easy to download. What's hard — unless you are on the cutting edge of physics — is actually understanding their content!

Preprints in the arXiv collection are classified by field (physics, astrophysics, mathematics, quantitative biology, and so forth) and, within each
field, by major subfields. Papers are submitted to the subfield archives and
are numbered by their date of arrival. As with journal articles, the titles of
preprints are omitted from citations. Here are some examples:

> Leinson, L. B., Pérez A. 2003, preprint, nucl-th/0312001 <http://www
> .arxiv.org/ PS_cache/nucl-th/pdf/0312/0312001.pdf>
> Watson, A. A. 2003, preprint, astro-ph/0312475

> or

> Watson, A. A. 2003, preprint (astro-ph/0312475)

The classification system is as simple as the papers are complex. Take the
Watson paper. It's in astronomy and astrophysics (astro-ph), was submitted in 2003 (03), in the 12th month (12), and was the 475th paper submitted
in its category that month (475). Hence, astro-ph/0312475.

For the Leinson article, I included the full URL, but that's not essential.
Professionals in the field know where to find arXiv preprints, either at the
main archive or mirror sites. It's sufficient to list the ID: nucl-th/0312001

Preprints like these should be cited and included in your reference list,
just like journal articles. Unpublished does not mean uncited.

12

MATHEMATICS AND COMPUTER SCIENCE CITATIONS

. . . .

Papers in mathematics and computer science use one of two citation styles. The first places an alphabetical reference list at the end of the paper. References in the text are given by bracketed numbers. The first reference might be [23], referring to the twenty-third item in the alphabetical list. The last reference in the article might be [2]. Specific pages are rarely mentioned, but if you need to, use this form: [23, p. 14]. Please use the set of positive integers.

A second system, based on the *Bulletin of the American Mathematical Society*, is often used by advanced mathematicians for publishable research. It, too, has an alphabetical reference list (a slightly different one), but what's unusual are the text references. Instead of bracketed numbers, this style uses abbreviations, based on the author's last name and date of publication. So an article by Hofbauer and Sandholm, published in *Econometrica,* volume 70 (2002), would be cited in the text as something like [HoSa02] or perhaps [HS02] or maybe just [HS]. It's your choice. This abbreviation also appears in the reference list, identifying the entry for Hofbauer and Sandholm's article. In the second table below, I show how to use this AMS *Bulletin* system.

Most books and articles are classified by subfield and uniquely identified in the Mathematical Reviews (MR) Database. Whichever citation system you use, you can include this MR number as the last item in each reference, after the date or page numbers. The MR Database is searchable through the American Mathematical Society's Web site at http://www.ams.org/mr-database.

If the article you are citing is available online, perhaps at the author's Web site, mention the URL just before the MR number. If there is no MR number, the Web page appears last.

In the following tables, I show standard mathematical citation forms. Many math journals don't stick to one format. Some use numerical citations for one article and AMS *Bulletin* style for the next. To add to the fun, they'll use the same style differently in different articles. One might list the author as R. Zimmer. The very next article (using the same style) lists the author as Zimmer, R. If I kept looking, I'd probably find one that calls him Bob Zimmer. One article puts the publication date in parentheses; the next one doesn't. In one, the reference list uses italics for every article title and regular type for journal names. The next one does exactly the opposite. Some use boldface for journal numbers, and others don't. Frankly, I don't think any of this matters very much, as long as you are consistent and your teacher is okay with it.

In the tables below, I've swept away these variations and idiosyncrasies. The tables use consistent rules, based on recent editions of major journals in mathematics and computer science.

Article titles and book chapters are italicized. Capitalize only the first word, the first word after a colon, and all proper nouns:

A. R. Conn and P. L. Toint, *An algorithm using quadratic interpolation for unconstrained derivative free optimization*

Book titles are capitalized normally and italicized:
Nonlinear Optimization and Applications

Journal titles are abbreviated but not italicized:
Ann. of Math.
Bull. Amer. Math. Soc.
Geom. Topol.
Trans. Amer. Math. Soc.

A full list of journal abbreviations, compiled by the American Mathematical Society, is available at http://www.ams.org/msnhtml/serials.pdf.

Publications by the same author are listed in the order of publication, beginning with the earliest. Use three em dashes to repeat an author's name, but do so only if *all* the authors are the same. For example:

[32] S. Kihara, *On an elliptic curve over Q(t) of rank ≥ 14*, Proc. Japan Acad. Ser. A Math. Science. 77 (2001), pp. 50-51 MR 2002a:11057.

[33] ———, *On an infinite family of elliptic curves with rank ≥ 14 over*

Q, Proc. Japan Acad. Ser. A Math. Science. 73 (1997), p. 32 MR
98d:11059.

[34] S. Kihara and M. Kenku, *Elliptic Curves* . . . .

MATHEMATICS: NUMBERED REFERENCE LIST (ALPHABETICAL ORDER)

Journal article

[1] J. Burkardt, M. Gunzburger, and J. Peterson, *Insensitive functionals, inconsistent gradients, spurious minima, and regularized functionals in flow optimization problems*, Int. J. Comput. Fluid Dyn. 16 (2002), pp. 171–185.

[2] I. D. Coope and C. J. Price, *Positive bases in numerical optimization*, Comput. Optim. Appl. 21 (2003), pp. 169–175.

[3] N. P. Strickland, *Finite subgroups of formal groups*, J. Pure Appl. Algebra 121 (1997), pp. 161–208.

[4] ——, *Gross-Hopkins duality*, Topology 39 (2000), pp. 1021–1033.

▸ Bracketed numbers go in the left margin. Articles are listed in alphabetical order, by author's name.

▸ If an author's name is repeated (and there are no new coauthors), then use three em dashes, followed by a comma. (Em dashes are simply long dashes, about the length of the letter "m." If for some reason, you can't find these em dashes, just use three hyphens.)

Online article

[#] M. Haiman, *Hilbert schemes, polygraphs, and the Macdonald positivity conjecture*, J. Amer. Math. Soc. 14 (2001), pp. 941–1006. Available at http://www.math .berkeley.edu/~mhaiman. MR 2002c:14008.

[#] J. Holt, *Multiple bumping of components of deformation spaces of hyperbolic 3-manifolds*, Amer. J. Math. 125 (2003), pp. 691–736. Available at http:// muse.jhu.edu/journals/american_journal_of _mathematics/v125/125.4holt.pdf.

Preprint

[#] J. S. Ellenberg, *Serre's conjecture over F_9*, preprint (2002), submitted for publication. Available at http:// www.math.princeton.edu/~ellenber/papers.html.

[#] J. Haglund, *Conjectured statistics for the q, t-Catalan*

Preprint (*continued*)	*numbers*, preprint (2003), to appear in Advances in Math. Available at http://www.math.upenn.edu/~jhaglund. [#] R. Miatello and R. Podesta, *The spectrum of twisted Dirac operators on compact flat manifolds*, preprint (2003). Available at arXiv, math. DG/0312004. ▸ In mathematics, as in physics, there's a large, easily accessible electronic archive of preprints available arXiv. The math collection is at http://www.arxiv.org/archive/math. You can cite either the entire URL for a preprint, as the reference below for L. W. Tu does, or you can simply list the archival number and say it is available at arXiv, as the reference for Miatello and Podesta does. [#] X. Sun, *Singular structure of harmonic maps to trees*, preprint (2001), published as *Regularity of harmonic maps to trees*, Amer. J. Math. 125 (2003), pp. 737–771. [#] R. Taylor, *On the meromorphic continuation of degree two L-functions*, preprint (2003). Available at http://abel.math.harvard.edu/~rtaylor/. [#] L. W. Tu, *A generalized Vandermonde determinant*, preprint (2003). Available at http://www.arxiv.org/PS_cache/math/pdf/0312/0312446.pdf.
Other unpublished papers	[#] J. S. Ellenberg, *Hilbert modular forms and the Galois representations associated to Hilbert-Blumenthal abelian varieties*, Ph.D. diss., Harvard University, 1998. [#] P. Hovland, *Automatic differentiation and its role in simulation-based optimization*, IMA Workshop, Minneapolis, MN, 2003. [#] M. J. D. Powell, *On the Lagrange functions of quadratic models that are defined by interpolation,* Tech. Rep. DAMTP 2000/NA10, Department of Applied Mathematics and Theoretical Physics, University of Cambridge, Cambridge, UK, 2000.
Book, one author	[#] S. Alinhac, *Blowup for Nonlinear Hyperbolic Equations, Progr. Nonlinear Differential Equations Appl.*, Vol. 17, Birkhäuser, Boston, 1995. [#] A. Weil, *Basic Number Theory*, Springer-Verlag, Berlin, 1995.

Book, multiple authors	[#] P. E. Gill, W. Murray, and M. H. Wright, *Practical Optimization*, Academic Press, London, 1981. ► If there are many authors, then name only the first and add "et al." Example: Gill et al., *Practical Optimization . . . .*
Book, multiple editions	[#] R. Fourer, D. M. Gay, and B. W. Kernighan, *AMPL: A Modeling Language for Mathematical Programming*, 2nd ed., Thomson/Brooks/Cole, Pacific Grove, CA, 2003.
Multivolume book	[#] R. Fletcher, *Practical Methods of Optimization*, 2nd ed., Vol. 2, Wiley and Sons, New York, 1980. [#] M. Reed and B. Simon, *Methods of Modern Mathematical Physics* I. *Functional Analysis*, Academic Press, New York, 1980. [#] G. W. Stewart, *Matrix Algorithms. Volume I: Basic Decompositions*, SIAM, Philadelphia, PA, 1998.
Article in multivolume book	[#] W. E. Hart, *A stationary point convergence theory of evolutionary algorithms*, in *Foundations of Genetic Algorithms 4*, R. K. Belew and M. D. Vose, eds., Morgan Kaufmann, San Francisco, CA, 1997, pp. 127–134.
Book, edited	[#] F. E. Browder (ed.), *Proc. Symposia in Pure Math., vol. 18, part 2*, Nonlinear Operators and Nonlinear Equations of Evolution in Banach Spaces, Amer. Math. Soc., Providence, 1976. [#] U. Hornung (ed.), *Homogenization and Porous Media*, Springer, Berlin, 1996.
Chapter in edited book	[#] A. R. Conn and P. L. Toint, *An algorithm using quadratic interpolation for unconstrained derivative free optimization*, in *Nonlinear Optimization and Applications*, G. Di Pillo and F. Giannessi, eds., Kluwer Academic/Plenum Publishers, New York, 1996, pp. 27–47. ► Notice that the chapter is capitalized like a sentence, but the book title is capitalized normally.

Software program	[#] T. G. Kolda, P. D. Hough, G. Gay, S. Brown, D. Dunlavy, and H. A. Patrick, *APPSPACK (Asynchronous parallel pattern search package)*; software available at http://software.sandia.gov/appspack.
	[#] *MultiSimplex 2.0*. Grabitech Solutions AB, Sundvall, Sweden, 2000; software available at http://www.multi simplex.com.

> ▸ When there is no author, as with this software program, alphabetize by its title.

Now, let's turn to the AMS *Bulletin* style. A few general points:

• To repeat an author's name, use three em dashes instead of the name. But do so only if *all* authors are the same.

• Capitalize only the first word (and proper nouns) for *article* titles. For book and journal titles, on the other hand, capitalize all important words; journal titles are also abbreviated.

• When the place of publication is contained in the publisher's name and is well known, then omit the place-name. Examples: Oxford UP, Cambridge UP, Princeton UP, and U Chicago P.

• To differentiate publications by the same author, include numbers after the initials. For example, assume you are citing one article published by J. Holt in 2002 and another in 2004. You could label them as [Ho1] and [Ho2], or as [Ho02] and [Ho04].

• To denote unpublished articles, you may add an asterisk if you wish, such as [Hop98*], but that is optional.

It may be helpful to see these AMS *Bulletin* citations used in an article text. Here are a couple of examples:

This question was posed by Pyber [Py3] and answered by Murray [Mu].

In [Bo98], uniform barriers are handled differently.

MATHEMATICS: AMS *BULLETIN* STYLE (ALPHABETICAL ORDER)

Journal article	[ATW02]	A.B. Ania, T. Tröger and A. Wambach: *An evolutionary analysis of insurance markets with adverse selection*, Games Econ. Behav. **40** (2002), 153–184.

> ▸ Initials such as A.B. have no spaces between them.

> - Articles and chapters are capitalized in sentence style. Titles of books and journals, on the other hand, are capitalized normally. Journal titles are abbreviated.

[Bo91]   I.M. Bomze: *Cross entropy minimization in uninvadable states of complex populations*, J. Math. Biol. **30** (1991), 73–87. MR **92j**:92012

> - There is no punctuation after the MR number.

Online article	[Ha01]	M. Haiman: *Hilbert schemes, polygraphs, and the Macdonald positivity conjecture*, J. Amer. Math. Soc. **14** (2001), 941–1006. Available at http://www .math.berkeley.edu/~mhaiman. MR **2002c**:14008
	[Ho03]	J. Holt: *Multiple bumping of components of deformation spaces of hyperbolic 3-manifolds*, Amer. J. Math. **125** (2003), 691–736. Available at http://muse.jhu.edu/journals/ american_journal_of_mathematics/v125/ 125.4holt.pdf.
Preprint	[BEV]	A. Bravo, S. Encinas and O. Villamayor: *A simplified proof of desingularization and applications*, preprint (2002). Available at http://arXiv.org/abs/ math/0206244.
Other unpublished papers	[Hop96]	M. J. Hopkins: *Course note for elliptic cohomology*, unpublished notes (1996).
	[Hop98]	——: *K(1)-local E*$_\infty$ *ring spectra*, unpublished notes (1998).
	[Mu]	S. Murray: *Conjugacy classes in maximal parabolic subgroups of the general linear group*. Ph.D. diss. (1999), University of Chicago.
Online book	[PU1]	F. Przytycki and M. Urbanski: *Fractals in the Plane — The Ergodic Theory Methods*. Available at http:// www.math.unt.edu/~urbanski, to appear in Cambridge UP.

> - Some authors add an asterisk to denote unpublished articles, for example: [PU1*]. The number 1 indicates that there are other cited books by the same coauthors, such as PU2.

Book, one author	[Cro3]	R. Cressman: *Evolutionary Dynamics and Extensive Form Games.* MIT Press, Cambridge, MA, 2003. ▸ If you are citing several works by Cressman, you could name them by their year of publication, such as [Cr98], [Cro2]; or you could name them [Cr1], [Cr2].
Book, multiple authors	[HaSe88]	J.C. Harsany and R. Selten: *A General Theory of Equilibrium Selection in Games.* MIT Press, Cambridge, MA, 1988. MR **89j**:90285
Book, multiple editions	[vD91]	E. van Damme: *Stability and Perfection of Nash Equilibria,* 2nd ed., Springer, Berlin, 1991. MR **95f**:90001
Multivolume book	[Rot]	E. E. Rothman: *Reducing Round-off Error in Chebyshev Pseudospectral Computations.* In: M. Durand and F. El Dabaghi (eds.), *High Performance Computing II.* Elsevier/North-Holland, Amsterdam, 1991, pp. 423–439.
Article in multivolume book	[Py3]	L. Pyber: *Group enumeration and where it leads us,* in *European Congress of Mathematics: Budapest July 22–26, 1996,* vol. 2. Birkhäuser, Basel, 1998. MR **99i**:20037
Book, edited	[DR98]	L.A. Dugatkin and H.K. Reeve (eds.): *Game Theory and Animal Behaviour.* Oxford UP, 1998.
	[Nao2]	J. Nash: *The Essential John Nash,* H.W. Kuhn and S. Nasar (eds.), Princeton UP, 2002. MR **2002k**:01044
Chapter in edited book	[Bo98]	I.M. Bomze: *Uniform barriers and evolutionarily stable sets.* In: W. Leinfellner, E. Köhler (eds.), *Game Theory, Experience, Rationality.* Kluwer, Dordrecht, 1998, pp. 225–244. MR **2001h**:91020

TEXT STYLE IN MATHEMATICS

Finally, all math papers (regardless of their citation format) have special rules governing the way to present standard terms such as theorems and proofs, as well as the way to present the text following these terms.

MATHEMATICAL TERM	PROPER FORMAT FOR THIS TERM	TEXT AFTER THE TERM
THEOREM	THEOREM or **Theorem**	*Italicized*
LEMMA	LEMMA or **Lemma**	*Italicized*
COROLLARY	COROLLARY or **Corollary**	*Italicized*
PROOF	*Proof*	Standard, no italics
DEFINITION	*Definition*	Standard, no italics
NOTE	*Note*	Standard, no italics
REMARK	*Remark*	Standard, no italics
OBSERVATION	*Observation*	Standard, no italics
EXAMPLE	*Example*	Standard, no italics

For more details, see Ellen Swanson, *Mathematics into Type*, updated by Arlene O'Sean and Antoinette Schleyer (Providence, RI: American Mathematical Society, 1999). *The Chicago Manual of Style*, chapter 14, provides an alternative guide to formatting. Either is fine as long as you are consistent.

BLUEBOOK LEGAL CITATIONS

• • • • • • • • • • • • • •

Legal citations are commonly based on *The Bluebook: A Uniform System of Citation*, published by the Harvard Law Review.[1] Recently, the Association of Legal Writing Directors developed an alternative manual for classroom use, *The ALWD Citation Manual.*[2] The two systems are similar but not identical.

Despite its simple and inviting name, the *Bluebook* is actually a detailed reference manual, and often a complicated one. Traditions of legal writing and referencing add to the complexity. A commonplace task like citing an article offers a good example of this complexity. Using standard *Bluebook* style, you need to use three different typefaces: ordinary Roman, *italics*, and SMALL CAPS. Take this article, which appears in volume 40 of the *Virginia Journal of International Law*, beginning on page 1103:

> Anne-Marie Slaughter, *Judicial Globalization*, 40 VA. J. INT'L L. 1103 (2000).

Not every legal journal follows these conventions, but many do and no other style is so widely used.[3] In the table of citations below, I'll concentrate on this standard version.

---

1. *The Bluebook: A Uniform System of Citation*, 17th ed. (Cambridge, MA: Harvard Law Review Association, 2000). By the way, the *Bluebook*'s citation for itself is

THE BLUEBOOK: A UNIFORM SYSTEM OF CITATION (Columbia Law Review Ass'n et al. eds., 17th ed. 2000).

2. Association of Legal Writing Directors and Darby Dickerson, *The ALWD Citation Manual: A Professional System of Citation*, 2d ed. (New York: Aspen Publishers, 2003).

3. Although the *Bluebook* is standard, many law reviews vary from it. There's nothing wrong with these variations, but we'll stick to the *Bluebook* style here to keep things as clear as possible.

Notice, too, that legal citations frequently use abbreviations. In fact, the *Bluebook* has page after page listing abbreviations for journals, courts, legislative documents, and so on. There no single online site with all these abbreviations, but some sites go part of the distance. The University of Washington Law Library has a helpful list of journal abbreviations at http://lib.law.washington.edu/cilp/abbrev.html. I have added a short list of abbreviations for other common legal terms at the end of this chapter.

Amid this complexity, there is at least one shortcut. You don't need to construct a bibliography. The first footnote gives complete information about the item.

INDEX OF *BLUEBOOK* CITATIONS IN THIS CHAPTER

LEGAL CITATIONS: *BLUEBOOK* STYLE

Journal article	Eric A. Posner & Adrian Vermeule, *Interring the Nondelegation Doctrine*, 69 U. Chi. L. Rev. 1721 (2002). ▸ Two authors are separated by "&." If there are three or more, normally list only the first, followed by "et al." ▸ The small caps used here for the journal title are found under Format/Font in Microsoft Word. Eugene Volokh et al., *The Second Amendment as Teaching Tool in Constitutional Law Classes*, 48 J. Legal Educ. 591, 595–98 (1998). ▸ Let's decode the citation for Volokh's article: it appears in volume 48 of the *Journal of Legal Education*, beginning on page 591. Within the article, I am citing pages 595–98. The same pagination format applies to court cases, laws, and other items. First list the document's opening page, then mention the specific pages you are citing.
Later citations	*See* Posner & Vermeule, *supra* note 99, at 1723. ▸ The *Bluebook* italicizes the term *see* because it is a "signaling term." There are many such terms, including *e.g.*, *cf.*, and *compare*. ▸ "*Supra* note 99" tells the reader that the full reference to Posner and Vermeule is given above at footnote 99. Of course, this could be easily said in English: cited in note 99. Doing so, however, might reduce the hourly billing rate. Id. at 1724–25. ▸ This refers to the same article as the previous note, but different pages.
Journal article, with quotation in footnote	Russell Korobkin, *Bounded Rationality, Standard Form Contracts, and Unconscionability*, 70 U. Chi. L. Rev. 1203 (2003) ("If anything, the dominance of form contracts over negotiated contracts has increased" over the past thirty years.). ▸ Notice that in legal citations, quotes within footnotes come after the citation and are placed in parentheses.
Online journal article	John J. Brogan, *Speak & Space: How the Internet Is Going to Kill the First Amendment as We Know It*, 8 Va. J.L. & Tech. 6 (2003), *at* http://www.vjolt.net.

François Brochu, *The Internet's Effect on the Practice of Real Property Law: A North American Perspective*, 2 J. INFO. L. & TECH. (2003), *at* http://elj.warwick.ac.uk/jilt/03-2/brochu.html.

Unpublished papers and theses	Cass R. Sunstein, *Why Does the American Constitution Lack Social and Economic Guarantees?*, University of Chicago, Public Law Working Paper No. 36 (Jan. 2003), *at* http://papers.ssrn.com/sol3/papers.cfm?abstract_id=375622.

William Landes, *Winning the Art Lottery: The Economic Returns to the Ganz Collection*, RECHERCHES ECONOMIQUES DE LOUVAIN (forthcoming). University of Chicago Law School, John M. Olin Law & Economics Working Paper No. 76 (May 1999) *at* http://papers.ssrn.com/sol3/papers.cfm?abstract_id=163770.

▸ If you know when a forthcoming paper will be published, include the year: (forthcoming 2004).

Gregory M. Heiser, Fictions of Sovereignty: Legal Interpretation and the Limits of Narrative (1998) (unpublished Ph.D. dissertation, Pennsylvania State University) *at* http://faculty-staff.ou.edu/H/Gregory.M.Heiser-1/Dissertation.PDF.

Note or comment in journal	Pintip Hompluem Dunn, Note, *How Judges Overrule: Speech Act Theory and the Doctrine of* Stare Decisis, 113 YALE L.J. 493 (2003).

▸ If the legal term *stare decisis* appeared in regular text, it would be italicized. When it appears as part of an italicized text, such as this note title, its typeface is reversed to normal Roman. The same is true for court cases, which are italicized in the regular text of an article and reversed in the citation.

Robert H. Sitkoff, Comment, *"Mend the Hold" and* Erie: *Why an Obscure Contracts Doctrine Should Control in Federal Diversity Cases*, 65 U. CHI. L. REV. 1059 (1998).

▸ If this were a book review, it would say "Book note" instead of "Comment."

▸ If there were no author listed for this comment, the citation would begin:

Comment, *"Mend the Hold" and* Erie . . . .

Book, one author	BRUCE ACKERMAN, WE THE PEOPLE: TRANSFORMATIONS (1998). ▸ Book authors' names are set in small caps. KENNETH W. DAM, THE RULES OF THE GLOBAL GAME: A NEW LOOK AT U.S. INTERNATIONAL POLICYMAKING 115–25 (2001). ▸ Refers to pages 115–25.
Book, multiple authors	DOUGLAS G. BAIRD ET AL., GAME THEORY AND THE LAW (1994). ▸ According to *Bluebook,* if there are more than two authors (as there are for this book), you should normally list only the first name followed by "et al." They make an exception, however, if you consider the other authors' names particularly relevant. In that case, the citation would be DOUGLAS G. BAIRD, ROBERT H. GERTNER & RANDAL C. PICKER, GAME THEORY AND THE LAW (1994).
Book, multiple editions	RICHARD A. POSNER, ECONOMIC ANALYSIS OF THE LAW (6th ed. 2003).
Book, single volume in multivolume work	2 RALPH H. FOLSOM, INTERNATIONAL BUSINESS TRANSACTIONS 76–92 (2d ed. 2002). ▸ This refers to volume 2, pages 76–92.
Book, edited	ECONOMIC ANALYSIS OF THE LAW: SELECTED READINGS (Donald A. Wittman ed., 2003).
Chapter in edited book	Michael Sandel, *What Money Can't Buy: The Moral Limits of Markets, in* 21 TANNER LECTURES ON HUMAN VALUES 89 (Grethe B. Peterson ed., 2000).
Reporters, court cases, and decisions	Marbury v. Madison, 5 U.S. 137 (1803). ▸ In the text itself, case names are italicized. After the first textual reference, they are usually referred to by the name of the first party: *Marbury.* Roe v. Wade, 410 U.S. 113 (1973). Woodson v. North Carolina, 428 U.S. 280, 305 (1976) (opinion of Stewart, J.).

United States v. Emerson, 270 F.3d 203, 260 (5th Cir. 2001).
- "F.3d" refers to the *Federal Reporter,* Third Series.

63 F.3d 160 (2d Cir. 1995), *cert. denied*, 516 U.S. 1184 (1996).
- In this citation, the Second Circuit's opinion was appealed to the Supreme Court, which declined to hear the case. One rule of legal citations is that if the case was subsequently appealed, enforced, vacated, or otherwise acted upon, you need to show that in your citation.

Marriage of Friedman, 122 Cal. Rptr. 2d 412 (Ct. App. 2002), *review denied*, No. S109408 (Cal. 2002).

Unpublished judicial opinions	Ecology Works v. Essex Insurance, No. 02-15658, 58 Fed. Appx. 714, 2003 U.S. App. LEXIS 4862 (9th Cir. Mar. 17, 2003). - Some federal opinions are unpublished and do not appear in the *Federal Reporter.* However, unpublished opinions issued by federal appeals courts since January 2001 are available in the privately published *Federal Appendix.* Some are also available on the courts' own Web sites.
Federal rules	FED. R. EVID. 501. - *Federal Rules of Evidence,* rule number 501. FED. R. CIV. P. 9. FED. R. CRIM. P. 32. U.S. SENTENCING GUIDELINES MANUAL § 2T1.1(b)(2) (1997).
Codification and restatement	RESTATEMENT (SECOND) OF CONFLICT OF LAWS § 82 (1971). RESTATEMENT (THIRD) OF THE FOREIGN RELATIONS LAW OF THE UNITED STATES §§ 401–404 (1987). - § means section; §§ is the plural.
Federal laws, statutes, constitution	U.S. CONST. art. I, § 8, cl. 3. - Refers to the U.S. Constitution, article 1, section 8, clause 3. U.S. CONST. amend. V ("No person shall be held to answer for a capital, or otherwise infamous crime . . . ."). Homeland Security Act of 2002, Pub. L. No. 107-296, § 223, 116 Stat. 2135; § 312, 116 Stat. 2176; § 871 116 Stat. 2243 (2002). Telecommunications Act of 1997, Pub. L. No. 104-104, 110 Stat. 56 (1996).

Federal laws, statutes, constitution (*continued*)	Exchange Act of 1934 § 23(a)(1), 15 U.S.C. § 78w (2000). North American Free Trade Implementation Act, Pub. L. No. 103-182, 107 Stat. 2057 (codified at 19 U.S.C. § 3301 (1993)).
Federal codes	42 U.S.C. § 2000e-2(a)(2). Freedom of Information Act, 5 U.S.C. § 552 (1966), *amended by* Pub. L. No. 104-231, 110 Stat. 3048 (1996).
Regulations and agency materials	Implementation of the Location Competition Provisions in the Telecommunications Act of 1996, 61 Fed. Reg. 45,476, 45,493 (Aug. 29, 1996). Promoting Wholesale Competition through Open Access Non-Discriminatory Transmission Services by Public Utilities; Recovery of Stranded Costs by Public Utilities and Transmitting Utilities, 75 F.E.R.C. ¶ 61,080, F.E.R.C. Stats. & Regs. 31,036, 61 Fed. Reg. 21,540 (May 10, 1996). Appropriate Framework for Broadband Access to the Internet over Wireline Facilities, 67 Fed. Reg. 9232 (proposed Feb. 28, 2002).
State and local laws, codes	CAL. HEALTH & SAFETY CODE § 11488.4(i)(3) (West 2001). CAL. PENAL CODE § 667(b)–(i), *amended by* 1994 Cal. Stat. 12 § 1 (legislative version effective Mar. 7, 2000). ILL. CONST. of 1970, art. 5, § 12 (expressly conferring upon the governor the power to reprieve death sentences). Washington State Medical Use of Marijuana Act, WASH. REV. CODE ch. 69.51A, 1999 c 2 (Initiative Measure No. 692, approved Nov. 3, 1998).
State court decisions	People v. Latona, 184 Ill. 2d 260, 277 (1998). Commonwealth v. Lockwood, 109 Mass. 323, 336 (1872).
Treaties	Agreement between the United States and Japan Concerning the Treaty of Mutual Cooperation and Security, Jan. 19, 1960, 11 U.S.T. 3420, 131 U.N.T.S. 83 (entered into force June 23, 1960). Protocol [No. 1] to the Convention for the Protection of Human Rights and Fundamental Freedoms, Mar. 20, 1952,

E.T.S. No. 9, 213 U.N.T.S. 262 (hereinafter "European Convention on Human Rights").

▸ Since there is no obvious way to shorten this lengthy title, the "hereinafter" phrase tells the reader how you will shorten it. A subsequent reference would read:

European Convention on Human Rights, *supra* note 132.

CONSOLIDATED TREATY ON EUROPEAN UNION, Oct. 2, 1997, 1997 O.J. (C 340) 145.

▸ Because this treaty effectively forms the EU constitution, its title is in small caps, as a constitution would be.

North American Free Trade Agreement (NAFTA), Dec. 17, 1992, 32 I.L.M. 605 (1993).

▸ I.L.M. = International Legal Materials

Arbitrations	NASD Code of Arbitration, art. 10332. ICC Arbitration Rules, art. 8(2).
Patent	U.S. Patent No. 3,819,921 (issued June 25, 1974). ▸ This was Texas Instruments' patent for the first handheld calculator.
Newspaper article	James Brooke, *Japan and Russia Working Hard to Build Economic Ties*, N.Y. TIMES, Jan. 23, 2004, at W1.
Book review	Stephen Labaton, *Click Here for Democracy*, N.Y. TIMES, May 13, 2001 (reviewing CASS SUNSTEIN, REPUBLIC.COM) *available at* http://www.nytimes.com/books/01/05/13/reviews/010513.13labatot.html. Michael Sullivan & Daniel J. Solove, *Can Pragmatism Be Radical? Richard Posner and Legal Pragmatism*, 113 YALE L.J. 687 (2003) (book review).
Interview	Telephone Interview with Sandra Day O'Connor, Associate Justice of the Supreme Court (Jan. 30, 2004).
Speeches and lectures	Associate Justice Anthony M. Kennedy, Speech at the American Bar Association Annual Meeting (Aug. 9, 2003), *at* http://www.supremecourtus.gov/publicinfo/speeches/sp_08-09-03.html.

Speeches and lectures (*continued*)	President George W. Bush, Statement on the Next Steps in Strategic Partnership with India (Jan. 12, 2004), 40 WEEKLY COMP. PRES. DOC. 61 (Jan. 19, 2004), *at* http://www.state.gov/p/sa/rls/pr/28109.htm.
Dictionaries and reference works	BLACK'S LAW DICTIONARY 241 (7th ed. 1999). *Claimant, n., in* BLACK'S LAW DICTIONARY 241 (7th ed. 1999). 12 MARTINDALE-HUBBELL LAW DIRECTORY PA53B (2004). ▸ Refers to volume 12, page PA53B, referring to lawyers in Pennsylvania. *Supreme Court of the United States, in* 10 WEST'S ENCYCLOPEDIA OF AMERICAN LAW 12–14 (1998). ▸ Refers to volume 10, pages 12–14. ▸ The *Bluebook* omits citations for dictionary definitions and encyclopedia references. This format is based on *Bluebook* guidelines for similar works.
Database	National Law Center for Inter-American Free Trade, Intellectual Property Treaties, InterAm Database, *at* http://www.natlaw.com/database.htm.
DVD or CD-ROM	PHILLIP B. TAYLOR, CONSTITUTIONAL LAW (PUBLIC LAW) (ICLS Law Lecture Series CD-ROM, n.d.). ▸ n.d. = no date given for the CD-ROM.
Government document	149 CONG. REC. H2051–53 (daily ed. Mar. 19, 2003). *U.S. Military Commitments and Ongoing Military Operations Abroad: Testimony Before the Senate Armed Services Comm.*, 108th Cong. (2003) (statement of Paul Wolfowitz, Deputy Defense Secretary), *at* http://www.senate.gov/~armed_services/statemnt/2003/September/Wolfowitz.pdf. *Human Cloning Prohibition Act of 2001: Hearings on H.R. 1644 Before the Subcomm. on Crime of the House Comm. on the Judiciary*, 107th Cong. (2001) (statement of Jean Bethke Elshtain), *at* http://www.house.gov/judiciary/elshtain_061901.htm. H.R. CONF. REP. NO. 104-458, at 201 (1996). THE NATIONAL SECURITY STRATEGY OF THE UNITED STATES OF AMERICA (Sept. 17, 2002), *at* http://www.whitehouse.gov/nsc/nss.pdf.

U.S. Census Bureau, U.S. Dept. of Commerce, STATISTICAL ABSTRACT OF THE UNITED STATES 15 (123d ed. 2003).
U.S. Census Bureau, U.S. Dept. of Commerce, CENSUS 2000 CONGRESSIONAL DISTRICT SUMMARY FILE DVD (Software Version): 108th Congress (2003).

UN documents	U.N. CHARTER art. 23, para. 1. S.C. Res. 1441 (Nov. 8, 2002). ▸ This is U.N. Security Council Resolution 1441, which found Iraq in "material breach" of previous resolutions. U.N. Doc. S/PV.4692, at 5 (2003) ("Regrettably, the 12,000 page declaration [by the Iraqi government], most of which is a reprint of earlier documents, does not seem to contain any new evidence that would eliminate the questions or reduce their number."). *Universal Declaration of Human Rights*, G.A. Res. 217A, pmbl., U.N. Doc. A/810, at 71 (1948), *at* http://www.unhchr.ch/udhr/lang/eng.htm.

International courts	Military and Paramilitary Activities In and Against Nicaragua (Nicar. v. U.S.), 1984 I.C.J. 392 (Nov. 26).

Foreign court decisions	Jaston & Co. v. McCarthy, [1998] 59 B.C.L.R.3d 168 (B.C.C.A.). ▸ B.C.L.R.3d = *British Columbia Law Reports*, Third Series ▸ B.C.C.A. = British Columbia Court of Appeal (Canada) Canadian Council of Churches v. The Queen & Others [1992] 1 S.C.R. 236. ▸ S.C.R. = *Supreme Court Reports* (Canada)

Web site and Web page	U.S. Dep't of State, *What the Secretary Has Been Saying*, *at* State Department Web Site, http://www.state.gov/secretary/rm/c11020.htm. ▸ The *Bluebook* (17th ed.) does not fully specify how to cite Web pages. Their treatment of older Telnet sites, however, places an individual Web page in italics and the larger site (of which it is part) in normal Roman type.

COMMON LEGAL SYMBOLS AND ABBREVIATIONS

admission	admis.	constitution	Const.	law	l.
affidavit	aff.	court	Ct.	paragraph	¶ or para.
affirm	affirm	department	dep't	paragraphs	¶¶ or paras.
affirmed	aff'd	district	dist.	preamble	pmbl.
affirming	aff'g	document	doc.	regulation	reg.
amendment	amend.	exhibit	ex.	reversed	rev'd
article	art.	federal	Fed.	rules	r.
association	Ass'n	government	gov't	section	§
brief	Br.	judge	J.	sections	§§
certiorari	cert.	judges	JJ.	title	tit.
commission	Comm'n	judgment	J.	versus	v.
company	co.	justice	J.		

Note: Capitalization often depends on context. Contractions such as dep't are *not* followed by a period.

EXPLANATORY PHRASES

In these abbreviations, I do not indicate italics or capitalization. However, explanatory phrases such as *enforced* or *affirmed* are always italicized. They are called explanatory phrases because they explain the history of judicial decisions. Some, such as *cert. denied* and *rev'd*, are also abbreviated. The *Bluebook* contains a complete list of abbreviations and explanatory phrases in sections T6–16, pages 302–49.

Cornell University Law School provides a valuable interactive list of abbreviations, explanatory phrases, and other legal topics at http://www.law.cornell.edu/citation/topics.htm. Another handy source is the 'Lectric Law Library at http://www.lectlaw.com/def.htm.

14

FAQS ABOUT *ALL* REFERENCE STYLES

• • • • • • • • • • • • • • •

WHAT SHOULD YOU CITE?

Do I need to cite everything I use in the paper?

Pretty much. Cite anything you rely on for data or authoritative opinions. Cite both quotes and paraphrases. Cite personal communications such as e-mails, interviews, or conversations with professors if you rely on them for your paper. If you rely heavily on any single source, make that clear, either with multiple citations or with somewhat fewer citations plus a clear statement that you are relying on a particular source for a particular topic.

There is one exception. Don't cite sources for well-known facts. It's overkill to footnote any authorities for the signing of the Declaration of Independence on July 4, 1776. There will be time enough to footnote them when you start discussing the politics of the Continental Congress.

How many citations does a paper have, anyway?

It varies and there is no exact number, but a couple per page is common in well-researched papers. More is fine. If there are no citations for several pages in a row, something's probably wrong. Mostly likely, you just forgot to include them. You need to go back and fix the problem.

How many different sources should I use?

That depends on how complicated your subject is, how intensively you've studied it, and how long your paper is. If it is a complex subject or one that is debated intensely, you'll need to reflect that with multiple sources — some to present facts, some to cover different sides of the issue. On the other hand, if it's a short paper on a straightforward topic, you might need only a couple of sources. If you are unsure, ask what your professor expects for your topic. While you're talking, you might also ask about the best sources to use.

In any case, don't base longer, more complex papers on two or three sources, even if they are very good ones. Your paper should be more than a gloss on others' work (unless it is specifically an analysis of that scholar's work). It should be an original work that stands on its own. Use a variety of sources and make sure they include a range of opinions on any controversial topic.

You certainly don't need to agree with all sides. You are not made of rubber. But, at least for longer papers and hotly debated topics, you need to show that you have read different views, wrestled with varied ideas, and responded to the most important points.

By the way, your footnotes can be negative citations, as well as positive. You are welcome to disagree openly with a source, or you can simply say, "For an alternative view, see . . . ."

WHAT GOES IN A CITATION?

Can I include discussion or analysis in footnotes?

Yes, for most styles, *except in the sciences.* Footnotes or endnotes are fine spots to add brief insights that bear on your paper topic but would distract from your narrative if they were included in the text. Just remember you still need to edit these discursive notes, just as you do the rest of your writing. And don't let them become a major focus of your writing effort. The text is the main event.

If you use in-text citations such as (Tarcov 2004) and want to add some explanatory notes, you'll have to add them as a special set of citations. They are usually marked with a superscript number.

If you are writing in the sciences and already using superscripts for the citation-sequence system, you're better off avoiding explanatory notes entirely. If you really need to include one or two, mark them with an asterisk or other symbol. In this system, you cannot use numbered citations for anything except references.

I sometimes use articles from *Time* or *Newsweek*. Should they be cited like journal articles or newspaper articles?

That depends on how long and how significant the articles are. Short pieces in newsweeklies are usually treated like newspaper articles. You can include the author, but you don't have to. Either way, short articles are not usually included in the bibliography. Major articles with author bylines are treated more like journal articles and are included in the bibliography.

Some styles, notably Chicago and *Bluebook* legal references, use shortened citations after the first citation for an item. What's the best way to shorten a title?

There are some standard ways. One is to use only the author's last name: Strunk and White instead of William Strunk Jr. and E. B. White. You also drop the initial article in the title and any other needless words. *The Elements of Style* becomes *Elements of Style*. Drop the edition number and all publishing information, such as the publisher's name. For articles, drop the journal title and volume. So:

Long form	[99]William Strunk Jr. and E. B. White, *The Elements of Style*, 4th ed. (New York: Longman, 2000), 12.
	[100]Stefan Elbe, "HIV/AIDS and the Changing Landscape of War in Africa," *International Security* 27 (Fall 2002): 159–77.
Short form	[199]Strunk and White, *Elements of Style*, 12.
	[200]Elbe, "HIV/AIDS."

The shortened title for Elbe's work might be confusing if your paper dealt mainly with HIV/AIDS and was filled with similar citations. For clarity, you might decide on an alternative short title such as Elbe, "Landscape of War."

If the title has two parts, put on your surgical gloves and remove the colon.

Long form	[99]Robert A. Kaster, *Guardians of Language: The Grammarian and Society in Late Antiquity* (Berkeley: University of California Press, 1988).
	[100]Kenneth Shultz and Barry Weingast, "The Democratic Advantage: Institutional Foundations of Financial Power in International Competition," *International Organization* 57 (Winter 2003): 3–42.
Short form	[199]Kaster, *Guardians of Language.*
	[200]Shultz and Weingast, "Democratic Advantage."

You might need to shorten a title by identifying a few key words. Take Francis Robinson, ed., *Cambridge Illustrated History of the Islamic World.* There is no single right way to shorten this, but the best title is probably: Robinson, *History of Islamic World.* (Note that Robinson is simply listed as the author; his title as editor is dropped.)

In the first full note, you can also tell readers how you will shorten a title.

After giving the full title for Senate Banking Committee hearings on terrorist money laundering, for instance, you might say: (subsequently called "2004 Senate hearings").

For legal citations, you would say (hereinafter called "2004 Senate hearings"). To shorten legal citations, you also omit any book or article titles. Give only the author's name and say where the first full note is. For example: *See* Rosenberg, *supra* note 3.

What about citing a work I've found in someone else's footnotes? Do I need to cite the place where I discovered the work?

This issue comes up all the time because it's one of the most important ways we learn about other works and other ideas. Reading a book by E. L. Jones, for example, you find an interesting citation to Adam Smith. As it turns out, you are more interested in Smith's point than in Jones's commentary, so you decide to cite Smith. That's fine — you can certainly cite Smith — but how should you handle it?

There's a choice. One way is to follow the paper trail from Jones's note to Adam Smith's text, read the relevant part, and simply cite it, with no reference at all to Jones. That's completely legitimate for books like Smith's that are well known in their field. You are likely to come across such works in your normal research, and you don't need to cite Jones as the guide who sent you there. To do that honestly, though, you have to go to the Smith reading and examine the relevant parts.

The rule is simple: *Cite only texts you have actually used and would have found in the normal course of your research,* not obscure texts used by someone else or works you know about only secondhand. You don't have to read several hundred pages of Adam Smith. You do have to read the relevant pages in Smith — the ones you cite. Remember the basic principle: *When you say you did the work yourself, you actually did it.*

Alternatively, if you don't have time to read Smith yourself (or if the work is written in a language you cannot read), you can cite the text this way: "Smith, *Wealth of Nations*, 123, as discussed in Jones, *The European Miracle.*" Normally, you don't need to cite the page in Jones, but you can if you wish. An in-text citation would look different but accomplish the same thing: (Smith 123, qtd. in Jones).

This alternative is completely honest, too. You are referencing Smith's point but saying you found it in Jones. This follows another, equally important principle: *When you rely on someone else's work, you cite it.* In this case, you are relying on Jones, not Smith himself, as your source for Smith's point.

Follow the same rule if Jones leads you to a work that is unusual or obscure *to you*, a work you discovered only because Jones did the detailed research, found it, and told you about it. For example, one of Jones's citations is to a 1668 book by Paul Rycaut, entitled *The Present State of the Ottoman Empire.* I'm not an expert on the Ottoman Empire and certainly would not have discovered that book myself. Frankly, I'd never even heard of it until Jones mentioned it. So I'd cite it as (Rycaut 54, cited in Jones). I can do that without going to the Rycaut book. On the other hand, if I were a student of Ottoman history and Jones had simply reminded me of Rycaut's work, I could cite it directly. To do that honestly, however, I would need to go to the Rycaut volume and read the relevant passage.

Some scholars, unfortunately, sneak around this practice. They don't give credit where credit is due. They simply cite Rycaut, even if they've never heard of him before, or they cite Smith, even if they haven't read the passage. One result (and it really happens!) is that Jones makes a mistake in his citation and the next scholar repeats the error. It's really a twofold blunder: an incorrect footnote and a false assertion that the writer used Smith as a source.

The specific rules here are less important than the basic concepts:

- Cite only texts you found in the normal course of your research and have actually used.
- Cite all your sources openly and honestly.

Follow these and you'll do just fine.

BIBLIOGRAPHY

Do I need to have a bibliography?

Yes, for all styles *except* complete Chicago notes and legal citations. If you use *Bluebook* or full Chicago citations, the first note for each item gives readers complete information, including the title and publisher, so you don't need a bibliography. (You are welcome to include a bibliography if you use Chicago style, but you don't have to, unless your professor requires it.)

All other styles require a bibliography for a simple reason. The notes themselves are too brief to describe the sources fully.

Should my bibliography include the general background reading I did for the paper?

The answer depends on how much you relied on a particular reading and which reference style you use. MLA, APA, and science bibliographies include only the works you have actually cited. Chicago-style bibliographies are more flexible and can include works you haven't cited in a footnote.

My advice is this: If a work was really useful to you, then check to make sure you have acknowledged that debt somewhere with a citation. After you've cited it once, the work will appear in your bibliography, regardless of which style you use. If a particular background reading wasn't important in your research, don't worry about citing it.

Does the bibliography raise any questions about my work?

Yes, readers will scan your bibliography to see what kinds of sources you used and whether they are the best ones. There are five problems to watch out for:

- Old, out-of-date works
- Bias in the overall bibliography
- Omission of major works in your subject
- Reliance on poor or weak sources
- Excessive reliance on one or two sources

These are not really problems with the bibliography, as such. They are problems with the text that become apparent by looking at the bibliography.

Old sources are great for some purposes, but antiquated for others. Many consider Gibbon's *Decline and Fall of the Roman Empire* the greatest historical work ever written. But no one today would use it as a major secondary source on Rome or Byzantium. Too much impressive research has been completed in the two centuries since Gibbon wrote. So, if you were writing about current views of Byzantium or ancient Rome, *Decline and Fall* would be out-of-date. Relying on it would cast a shadow on your research. On the other hand, if you were writing about great historical works, eighteenth-century perspectives, or changing views about Byzantium, using Gibbon would be perfectly appropriate, perhaps essential.

"Old" means different things in different fields. A work published ten or fifteen years ago might be reasonably current in history, literature, and some areas of mathematics, depending on how fast those fields are changing. For a discipline moving at warp speed like genetics, an article might be out-of-date within a year. A paper in molecular genetics filled with citations from 1992 or even 2002 would cast serious doubt on the entire project. Whatever your field, you should rely on the best works and make sure they have not been superseded by newer, better research.

Bias, omission of key works, and overreliance on a few sources reveal other problems.[1] Bias means you have looked at only one side of a multifaceted issue. Your bibliography might indicate bias if it lists readings on only one side of a contested issue. Omitting an authoritative work not only impoverishes your work; it leaves readers wondering if you studied the topic carefully.

The remedy for all these problems is the same. For longer, more complex papers, at least, you need to read a variety of major works in your subject and indicate that with citations.

However long (or short!) your paper, make sure your sources are considered solid and reliable. Your professors and teaching assistants can really help here. They know the literature and should be valuable guides.

QUOTATIONS

I am using a quotation that contains a second quote within it. How do I handle the citation?

Let's say your paper includes the following sentence:

> According to David M. Kennedy, Roosevelt began his new presidency "by reassuring his countrymen that 'this great nation will endure as it has endured, will revive and will prosper. . . . The only thing we have to fear . . . is fear itself.'"

Of course, you'll cite Kennedy, but do you need to cite *his* source for the Roosevelt quote? No. It's not required. In some cases, however, your readers will benefit from a little extra information about the quote within a quote. You can easily do that in your footnote or endnote:

[99] Kennedy, *Freedom from Fear*, 134. The Roosevelt quote comes from his 1933 inaugural address.

I am quoting from some Spanish and French books and doing the translations myself. How should I handle the citations?

Just include the words "my translation" immediately after the quote or in the citation. You don't need to do this each time. After the first quotation,

---

1. Ralph Berry, *The Research Project: How to Write It* (London: Routledge, 2000), 108–9.

you can tell your readers that you are translating all quotes yourself. Then cite the foreign-language text you are using.

In some papers, you might want to include quotes in both the original and translation. That's fine. Either the translation or the original can come first; the other follows in parentheses or brackets. For instance:

> In Madame Pompadour's famous phrase, "Après nous, le déluge." (After us, the flood.) As it turned out, she was right.

ELECTRONIC MATERIALS AND MICROFILM

Some citations list "microfilm." Others list "microform" or "microfiche." What's the difference? Do I need to mention any of them in my citations?
They are all tiny photographic images, read with magnifying tools. Libraries use these formats to save money and storage space for large document collections. *All* these images are called *microforms,* no matter what material they are stored on. When they are stored on reels of film, they're called *microfilm.* When they are stored on plastic sheets or cards, they're called *microfiche.*

When you use materials that have been photographically reduced like this, you should say so in the citation, just as you do for Web sites or electronic information. (If the microforms simply reproduce printed material exactly, some citation styles allow you to cite the printed material directly. But you are always safe if you mention that you read it on microfilm or microfiche. The same is true for citing print items that are reproduced electronically.)

The URL I'm citing is long and needs to go on two lines. How do I handle the line break?
Here's the technical answer. If the URL takes up more than one line, break *after* a

- slash
- double slash

break *before* a

- period
- comma
- question mark
- tilde (~)
- ampersand (&)
- hyphen

- underline
- number sign

Here are some examples:

Full URL	http://www.charleslipson.com/index.htm
Break after slash	http://www.charleslipson.com/ index.htm
Break before other *punctuation*	http://www.charleslipson .com/index.htm

These "break rules" apply to all citation styles.

There's a rationale for these rules. If periods, commas, or hyphens come at the end of a line, they might be mistaken for punctuation marks. By contrast, when they come at the beginning of a line, they are clearly part of the URL. To avoid confusion, don't add hyphens to break long words in the URL.

You can produce such breaks in two ways. One is to insert a line break by pressing the shift-enter keys simultaneously, at least on Windows-based systems. Alternatively, you can insert a space in the URL so your word-processing program automatically wraps the URL onto two lines. (Without such a space, the word processor would force the entire URL onto one line.)

Even though you are technically allowed to break URLs before periods,

---

Tips on citing Web pages: As you take notes, write down the
- URL for the Web site or Web page
- Name or description of the page or site
- Date you accessed it

Writing the name or description of a Web site is useful because if the URL changes (as they sometimes do), you still can find it by searching.

As for the access date, some citation styles, such as APA and MLA, require it. Others, such as the *Chicago Manual of Style*, make it optional. They tell you to include it only when it's relevant, such as for time-sensitive data.

If sites are particularly useful, add them to your "favorites" list. If you add several sites for a paper, create a new category (or folder) named for the paper and drop the URLs into that. A folder will gather the sites in a single location and keep them from getting lost in your long list of favorites.

commas, and hyphens, I avoid such breaks because these punctuation marks are easy to overlook and confuse readers. Instead, I try to break only after a slash or double slash, and then only when I am printing the final version of the paper. When I'm sending it electronically, I try to avoid breaks altogether. That way, the recipient will have "live" hyperlinks to click on.

SCIENCE CITATIONS

In the sciences, some citations include terms like DOI, PII, and PMID. What are they? Do I need to include them in my citations?
They identify articles within large electronic databases. Just like other parts of your citations, they help readers locate articles and data you have used. In fact, you may use them yourself to return to an article for more research.

Not every scientific journal includes them in citations or lists them for its own articles. Some do; some don't. My advice: When you do research, write the numbers down and consider including them in your own citations. They appear at the very end of each citation, right after the pagination and URL.

What do the various letters mean? DOI stands for digital object identifier. It's an international system for identifying and exchanging digital intellectual property. Like a URL, it can be used to locate an item. Unlike a URL, it remains the same, even if the item is moved to a new location.

PII stands for publisher item identifier. It, too, identifies the article and can be used for search and retrieval.

PMID appears in many medical and biological journals. It stands for PubMed identification. The PubMed database includes virtually all biomedical journals plus some preprints. It is available online at www.ncbi.nlm .nih.gov/entrez and has a tutorial for new users. This invaluable database was developed by the National Center for Biotechnology Information at the National Library of Medicine.

Other specialized fields have their own electronic identifiers. MR, for example, refers to articles in the Mathematical Reviews database. Physics has identifying numbers for preprints (prepublication articles), which classifies them by subfield.

You are not required to list any of these electronic identifiers in your citations, but doing so may help you and your readers.

In the sciences, I'm supposed to abbreviate journal titles. Where do I find these abbreviations?

The easiest way is to look at the first page of the article you are citing. It usually includes the abbreviation and often the full citation for the article. You can also go to various Web sites assembled by reference librarians, listing journal abbreviations in many fields. One useful site is "All That JAS: Journal Abbreviation Sources," compiled and maintained by Gerry McKiernan, Science and Technology Librarian and Bibliographer at Iowa State, http://www.public.iastate.edu/~CYBERSTACKS/JAS.htm.

ACKNOWLEDGMENTS

. . . .

Since this book covers citations and academic honesty across the university, it was essential to speak with specialists from different fields. I was fortunate to receive advice on science labs from Tom Christianson, Nancy Schwartz, and Paul Streileman, (biological sciences), Vera Dragisich (chemistry), and Stuart Gazes (physics). All of them head lab programs at the University of Chicago. Diane Herrmann, who heads the undergraduate major in mathematics, offered a number of valuable comments about study groups. So did biologist Michael LaBarbera, who reviewed the chapter on academic honesty. For language learning, I spoke with Vincent Bertolini, Helma Dik, and Peter White, all at Chicago, and Robert Kaster at Princeton. For honor codes, I spoke with Susan Pratt and Keir Lieber, both of Notre Dame. Gerald Rosenberg, my colleague at Chicago and an expert in both law and politics, told me which legal citations would be most useful to students. James Marquardt, of Lake Forest College, offered thoughtful ideas about class participation. Physicist Thomas Rosenbaum, the University of Chicago's vice president for research, gave helpful comments on several chapters.

On all these issues, I spoke with students. I'd particularly like to thank Erik Cameron, an undergraduate at Reed College, and John Schuessler, a graduate of Notre Dame, for their thoughts on honor codes; Jonathan Grossberg, an undergraduate at Cornell, for his suggestions about effective study groups; and Jennifer London, a graduate student at Chicago, for her ideas about learning languages.

I checked all citation materials with experts, beginning with editors at the *Chicago Manual of Style*. I particularly wish to thank Linda Halvorson, who improved every aspect of this work and was a joy to work with. Jenni Fry offered very useful, detailed comments on all citation issues. For science citations, I was assisted by editors who supervise style manuals for two professional associations: Janet Dodd (chemistry), and Karen J. Patrias and Peggy Robinson (biological sciences). For astrophysics and astronomy, I received help from Sharon Jennings. Leslie Keros carefully reviewed the chapter on *Bluebook* legal citations. Peggy Perkins, one of the key editors for the *Chicago Manual of Style*, offered numerous ideas to improve the text and read the citation chapters with special care. William S. Strong, who handles copyright law for the University of Chicago Press, and Perry Cartwright, who handles contractual rights for the Press, offered wise counsel on the complex issues of plagiarism. Finally, the manuscript editor, Erin DeWitt, went through the entire volume with meticulous attention.

On general issues of academic honesty, I spoke with advisers, counselors, and deans who handle these issues every day. Special thanks go to Susan Art, the University of Chicago's Dean of Students, and Jean Treese, Associate Dean of Students and longtime head of the college's Orientation Program.

In their different jobs, they all promote genuine learning and honest accomplishments, the heart of a college education. Their generous help made this book possible.

INDEX

· · · · · · · · · · · ·

Abbreviations used:

ACS   American Chemical Society
AIP   American Institute of Physics
AMA   American Medical Association
AMS   American Mathematical Society
APA   American Psychological Association
Bluebook *Bluebook: A Uniform System of Citation*
Chicago   *The Chicago Manual of Style*
CSE   Council of Science Editors
MLA   Modern Language Association